Over the Rainbow

God's Eye
for the Gay Guy

a Story of Love and Hope...

a Message from
The Wonderful Wizard of Oz...

Angel WillSon

Over the Rainbow–God's Eye for the Gay Guy
©2017 Angel Willson

PRINTED IN THE USA

ISBN-13: 978-0692895320
ISBN-10: 0692895329

Dorothy's Club
P.O. Box 10275
Spokane, WA 99209
dorothysclub@yahoo.com
www.dorothysclub.org

2 3 4 5 6 7 8 9 10
Second Printing, 2017

Copies may be purchased by contacting the above. Available in bulk pricing for larger quantity orders.

Table of Contents

Acknowledgments

I want to thank David Mitchell for all his time and work with art design and graphic work, as well as for the encouragement and empowerment to me in this wonderful endeavor to reveal God's amazing love to people through this book.

I'd also like to thank Sarah Hodgman for her labors to help me complete this work with her editing support, prayers and encouragement.

Thanks to Suzanne Rivers for her encouragement to me and her work with me on my pre-editing. I'd also like to thank a friend of mine, Annie Pauletto, for key times of processing that were encouraging to me.

Many thanks to Cal Pierce and the Spokane International Healing Rooms for giving me a warm loving place to write this book. Also I'm grateful for all the love shown to me, the encouragements, prayers and support towards God's heart of love and healing.

Thanks to Meri Crouley, of Meri Crouley Ministries, who has brought me back to Hollywood to release this amazing grace message to Christians as well as to LGBT people in California.

I want to thank especially Pastor Jim, my long time pastor from my hometown, Spokane, who has believed in me since 1985, who has taught me marvellous things and who has been there for me in the deepest times of struggle, and with me through the most important transitions of my Yellow Brick Road pathway to maturity and fulfilled purpose in God's plan for me.

Thank you to Richard Church, Harold Eberle, Patrick McCluskey and Michael Danforth for faith in God's work in my life, for your life-changing encouragement, teachings, and friendship.

I cannot express how important, healing and significant it was for me to receive spiritual words from God from those who operated in the prophetic ministry. I have been a recipient of hundreds of prophetic words from people who didn't know me, about my past, present and future. This book and this ministry have been encouraged, empowered and literally birthed through these prophetic words. Here is a list of some specific prophets that have impacted my life through their prophetic ministries: Todd Bentley, Shawn Bolz, Kim Clement, Royal Cronquist, Meri Crouley, Michael Danforth, Dave Davis, Harold Eberle, Clarice Fluitt, Toni Kemp, Patricia King, Larry Randolph, Timothy Snodgrass, Jim White. Thank you for your words and ministry to me.

Thank you to Pastor Robert Douglas from Agape-COGIC in Tacoma for helping me through some tough times and getting me back on my feet again!

And thanks also to many in the body of Christ who ministered to me in the gifts of the Spirit throughout the years. I couldn't have made it without all of you!

Thank you to my adoptive mother in Spokane, who chose me. God caused you to choose me and I love and honor you as your son. He has also put HIS love in my heart for you. I also choose you! You are a wonderful gift from God to me.

Thank you to my birth mother for taking the higher path, to give me up to someone who you felt would give me a better life instead of the alternative option that others advised you to do. Thank you for the gift of life.

I'm grateful to both my adoptive mother and birth mother. You both gave me an inheritance in many ways, that empowered and launched me into the destiny that God called me to. You gave birth to and raised up an angel of God's love. Your love and sacrifices shall help bring God's love to multitudes.

I want to thank from the bottom of my heart, my dearest friend of all... **Grace Wilson.** Words cannot express the deepest gratitude that I have for your godly role modelling in my life. I am thankful for your loyal faith that God gave you to help me on my journey. Thank you for the years of grace, which completely suits your name which have given me faith and courage to go forward, especially the many times when I felt that I failed or couldn't bear the pains of life anymore. You chose to identify with me and this cause for the love of God and suffered for the hope and healing of multitudes of people of God and the LGBT community.

Introduction

The cover of this book is from a picture of me walking over the West Hollywood LGBT Rainbow crosswalk where I had a spiritual awakening on Santa Monica Boulevard, at the age of 19 at the Gay Pride Parade. That was its name then. It was at this approximate location that I had an experience that changed the rest of my life.

The LGBT rainbow colors weren't part of the pavement on Santa Monica Blvd., like it is now. 30 years later after this divine visitation, I revisited this location to discover the LGBTQ rainbow mixed into the pavement at the intersection. This is a parabolic, and factual autobiography of my life. This is my journey over one side of the LGBT rainbow to the other side, where the pot of gold is!

It's very fitting, writing largely to LGBT friends, to spiritually transgender myself, using Dorothy, as a metaphor. I'm using her as a type of us all that not only desire to get over the rainbow, but how to walk with resilience and perseverance in faith through the trials, attacks and temptations, that bring spiritual transformation into spiritual Christ-likeness, that happens on our Yellow Brick Road. Witches, Munchkins, Monkeys and Wizards are all metaphors to represent supernatural realities and entities from different spiritual dimensions...either from the Kingdom of Light from God or the dark, and false light of evil including the religious kingdom of Satan. The Bible talks about the battles for the hearts of humanity to know Christ and His love is due to spiritual evil forces of darkness in spiritual realms blinding the eyes of unbelievers (Ephesians 6:12) Satan's ultimate war for humanity is for us to not know who we really are, because when we do, heaven comes back to earth. Our destiny is heaven, but our assignment is bringing heaven to earth! (Bill Johnson). Our battle is that of identity. This is a designer pathway that God has created for each of his LGBT Dorothys. I call us Dorothy's Club. This journey takes Dorothy, who, according to the original book, *The Wonderful Wizard of Oz* begins as an orphan. She's adopted into the relative's family. She feels out of touch with herself, others and God. She doesn't understand nor is she understood. She is unenlightened. I also have been adopted out since birth and felt much the same as Dorothy. My adoptive mother and father bought me a book called, *The Chosen Baby*, when I was around four years old, to help me psychologically and emotionally adapt to being adopted, meaning chosen, instead of rejected. This book, *Over the Rainbow-God's Eye for the Gay Guy* carries the theme of *The Chosen Baby* throughout my story. I was told "Chosen" before Christ and after Christ, but the promise didn't play out in my families (both natural and spiritual) like I expected it to. I had to go through disillusionment many times, to discover reality. I had to discover what wasn't in order to discover what was. I did finally understand what it meant to be "Chosen." I hope this book helps you to discover how chosen you really are, especially if you don't feel chosen or believe that you're chosen at all.

Then through a storm and a rainbow, Dorothy is translated to another dimension called Oz, which metaphorically speaking in this book, represents the spiritual heavenly realms. I'm weaving my life through the metaphors of this story as a modern day parable. Jesus spoke in parables often so that those with hearts seeking truth, would see, hear and understand. Parables sift out those who have hearts, from those who don't. A parable, though, can cause a heart to seek for the truth, and thus be healed by the revelations they contain. God searches the hearts and hears the prayers and cries of Dorothy, played by adored Judy Garland, singing the song/prayer, "Somewhere Over the Rainbow" with the words "where troubles melt like lemon drops and where bluebirds fly." If you haven't read the book, *The Wonderful Wizard of Oz*, or seen the movie, please do so before you read this book. It may be difficult to understand if you haven't. You can read the book, *The Wonderful Wizard of Oz* free online, and/or purchase the movie, the *Wizard of Oz*.* The stories do diverge, but contain the similar story. My stories

*This book is not intended to be another version of the book or movie. I am just using the metaphors of the book and movie to explain my life experience and how God transformed me through the years. This is solely my interpretation of the themes for the purpose of sharing my journey and helping others. I do not claim nor wish to imply that these ideas are objectively in these works or represent the intent of the various creators. The book and movie provide wonderful entertainment value implicitly which I encourage all to enjoy.

are true and simple to understand and some of it is embroidered through the symbols. Real men during the times of Moses and Solomon did the work of embroidery, creating the colorful curtains in the temples and tabernacles of God. This book is spiritual embroidery. God gave me a sense of humor and I'm a horse of a different color.

This book is anointed with fresh oil from God according to Psalm 23 in the Old Testament, which has spiritually oiled my heart similar to the Tin Woodman, to express God's love to the LGBT community. I discovered throughout my journey much of Who and what God was, and what God wasn't. I had to get my own understanding as I studied the scriptures coupled with divine experience. The Bible wasn't my experience. It's only a book that talks about how to have your own experiences and relationship with the triune God...the Father, the Son and the Holy Spirit. I also found that there are seven more spirits of God that are before His Throne who also represent Who He is in the books of Isaiah and Revelations! Seven Spirits are also connected with the seven colors of the rainbow. There may be some concepts and experiences that may be hard to believe or understand, due to your own spiritual perceptions or background, so just receive what your heart wants and shelve the rest. In God's original rainbow, there is a seventh color called Indigo, which, according to *The Rainbow God* by Johnny Enlow, means spiritual revelation. I'm sharing with you about this seventh color that may be a key for many to be complete in their true Rainbow Identity.

> *That which we have seen, touched, felt and experienced, we now announce to you also, in order that you also may have fellowship in these experiences with us, and this fellowship with us is fellowship with the Father and with His Son Jesus Christ.*
> *1 John 3-5*

These spiritual experiences are to be transferred to you in God's special way as well as to be experienced through thoughtful and prayerful reading.

This book is not a 12 step program out of homosexuality, but a one step program to become a L.over of G.od B.eing T.rue....I am an "aint" and Jesus is the S which makes - Saint! A worm with wings...a butterfly. "If a man be in Christ, He has become a New Creation. Old identities and nature has passed away. Behold all things have become new!" - 2 Corinthians 5:17 (paraphrased)

A guest speaker at a church, named Jim, who didn't know anything about me, walked up to me and told me that God revealed to him that I was writing a book. He then said that a "scribe angel" was sent from God to help me with it. He then stated that he saw God kissing this book.

I pray that you will experience God's kiss to your heart while you're reading this. I have shared many of my failures, sins, and weaknesses so that you will take courage to not faint and give up on your Yellow Brick Road Journey. Romans declares that kindness leads us to surrender our will to God's love and plan. It also states that where sin abounds, grace super- abundantly abounds to more than match our failures, confusion and struggles in life. As the famous song goes, "Amazing Grace, how sweet the sound, that saved a wretch like me. I once was lost, but now am found. T'was blind but now I see!" Jesus shed enough blood for you, and gives you His indwelling Holy Spirit in order to walk with our head held high in the process of going from shame to favor. From ashes to beauty and from despair to exceedingly great joy. He was the Phoenix that died in the flames of crucifixion, and rose from the dead with healing powers in his tears. Jesus saved me from myself and from some of His followers, but poured out his love in my heart for us all. I didn't give up or give in, but paid the price to let Him complete a good work in me, so that I could pour out his unfathomable love through this book and my life to His favored and chosen ones, the LGBT community to complete them in Christ.

God, the heavenly Father sent His Son, Jesus to us to complete the broken rainbow and offers us a ride that no performance-based religion could possibly ever come near to. He has forgiven us of our sins and heals us of our dis-eases! He crowns us with love and compassion. (Psalm 103)

Chapter 1

Dorothy, Toto and Auntie Em

The story of the Wizard of Oz as most know, is about a young girl named Dorothy who lives on a rural farm in Kansas with her Auntie Em and uncles. The story never explains anything about Dorothy's biological parents. The original book says that Dorothy was an orphan.[1] This means she was "adopted" by her relatives.

Auntie Em and I, the Chosen Baby

In 1964 I was given up for adoption at birth. I never knew where I came from or anything about my birth parents until the age of 24. It was a supernatural encounter orchestrated by God, Himself, who guided me to my birth mother. I will share about this in a later chapter.

When a baby is adopted it is indeed chosen to be brought into a loving family committed to stewarding the proper formation of that child's sense of worth, identity, acceptance and destiny.

My adoptive parents had a four-year-old daughter and adopted me as a baby so she would have a brother. Two years later they would have another little girl. My first years of life until about the age of five, to me were full of wonder. My mom, who I absolutely adored, would read to me from a book called *The Chosen Baby*. It was full of pictures of loving, caring parents and

---

1 Baum, L. Frank. *The Wonderful Wizard of Oz*. The Project Gutenberg EBook. 1900. Web. <http://www.gutenberg.org/files/55/55-h/55-h.htm>.

siblings with a story of a happy family thrilled with the addition of this new adopted baby. Because of that book and how she so sweetly read it to me over and over again, I had no insecurities regarding my adoption. I trace the theme of the "Chosen Baby" throughout my story.

Dorothy Has a "Good Heart"

Metaphorically I am using Toto in my story to represent Dorothy's heart of truth. Children are born with this innocent heart until the world and those around them influence it to be hardened, if not Toto-lly destroyed (pun intended).

As a child I was deeply sensitive, caring, happy and gay, but not in the homosexual way...yet. I loved animals such as dogs, cats, and the boyish creatures such as lizards, frogs and turtles. In fact everyone in my family loved animals. As time went on, I think we all needed them more to cope with the family drama, and there was a lot!

Being one who was fun loving with good intentions, my Grandma Nan would say I had a "good heart" even when I made mistakes that others would criticize me over. My family would make fun of me, ridiculing me with those words. It felt much like Dorothy with Miss Gulch who was trying to destroy her little dog Toto. Grandma Nan cared about my Toto. She was my protector and I found refuge and comfort when I was around her because my heart felt safe with her. She was a great comfort zone for many of the family members. I think everyone felt as though they were her favorite, and we probably all were.

Many years later after I had received Christ, I had the privilege of praying with her to receive Jesus as her Lord and Savior. When she died I was invited by some relatives to officiate her funeral and was able to bring an inspirational message of Christ to family and friends.

Dorothy's Home Life

Dorothy is adopted into an American farm culture where basic needs were provided, but she was loved in a rather limited way. No one seemed to understand her sensitive, tender heart and although it was "good," her heart wasn't heard. Those around her were busy with their own stuff, responsibilities and interests.

My life felt like Dorothy's. My dad and I didn't have much in common at all. I tried but he didn't engage with me. I wanted a relationship with my dad and for the two of us to participate in each other's world. He was my idol. His idols were sports heroes. I felt invisible. He played catch with me once but only under the coaxing of my mom. I remember my mom calling out the family to watch the freak show of dad doing something with his son. I say that because it was embarrassing for me to have my mom make such a big deal out of my personal time with my Dad play-ing catch. I just wanted to do it together because I was his son, not so that it could be the news of the year. He went with me one time as a host on a Boy Scout camp about. That was a good memory. I needed my peers to see that I actually had a dad. I also remember him coming home in what was called an "Aqua Car." It was the kind of car you could drive into a lake and it would become a boat. He picked me up at home to go for a ride. I was elated to be in this amazing cool car with my dad, being with him and doing something with him. I had visions of us going to the lake to test it out. Instead he drove us to a tavern and I sat in this cool car while he went in to drink and hang out with his friends. He took me golfing once. I had never played before and because I hit the grass too many times he got mad and never took me again. He also took me fishing with his friends but I was left on the dock with a fishing pole while they took off to enjoy a day on the lake for many hours. I stood alone on that dock disillusioned and wondering why I had a dad who chose me but didn't want me.

My dad loved to hunt and fish. He went out with his friends and took the family out many times. I wanted to be with him and his friends outside of just the family. I wanted to feel special to him. I never learned to hunt and do "man things." I couldn't help my dad work on cars because he would yell at me for not knowing how to help correctly. He lacked patience and didn't know how to be a relational father to me. He was a good provider though. I have to say that compared to many people, he spoiled us.....possibly rotten. All the manly things that fathers help their sons take interest in through relationship and participation, I never got. I guess I could say my dad caused me to relate mostly to females through his failure to father me. I ended up feeling more like a girl than a guy. Because of that my own voice in my head began to sound to me like a female. The male wasn't being pulled out of me by my Dad. Nor did I have any brothers. I can see, at least one reason why some boys can feel and think they're girls.

My mom was a legal secretary and loved typing, so I became great at typing. She was very creative with crafts and floral de-sign. She knew how to organize things well and did a great job. Outside of the way she treated me at times, which could be a bit over the top, I loved everything about her. She was and still is an amazing woman. Because she was the only one who wanted to adopt me, which I discovered later, my relationship was mostly with her. We did a lot together.

My older sister often treated me as though I wasn't chosen, at least by her. One day while she was babysitting me, she put curlers in my hair and locked me out on the front porch. I was horrified and humiliated before the outside world. She and my younger sister would sometimes do things against me to make my life miserable. I actually loved my older sister and looked up to her and desperately wanted her love and acceptance. My younger sister and I were much closer but she sometimes got caught up into the meanness. I longed to be close to each of them. They were dear to my heart and still are to this day.

I am so thankful that at a very young age my mom sent me to a Lutheran kindergarten. That was where I first heard about the Good Shepherd in Psalm 23. I also liked to go to church sometimes and was drawn to Jesus. Many of my relatives were LDS, and would take me to church with them. I almost became a Mormon because of what appeared to be healthier family dynamics. Sometimes my Mom and I would go to a denominational church on a holiday or when we felt like it, which wasn't that often. Because I loved to sing so much I would join a church choir. The message of Christ went into my heart through these times. I travelled with a youth group called Emanon one year as a teenager. We would sing songs from the 1970's rock opera movie, *Godspell*. I sang a duet called, "It's All for the Best." I loved the songs from the Jesus people rock operas! I love Freddie Mercury from Queen and wished I had developed a voice like his. I have a good voice, though, which developed because of the choirs and plays I was in.

The first musical I performed in was *The Sound of Music* at a high school. I played the role of Kurt Von Trapp. When I got a part in my first musical, I felt for the first time in school, that I found my peeps. I found my niche. Theatre! Musicals! I found other guys, similar to me that shared similar family stories of rejection who were also in the plays. I didn't feel completely outcast and stigmatized any more. The hills were becoming alive, with the sound of music! When the movie, *Saturday Night Fever* came out in the 70's, I discovered not only disco, but dancing! I've never stopped. I found the gay dance clubs from Spokane, Washington, to Seattle, Portland, San Francisco, down to West Hollywood, California! Because I grew up in taverns that my Dad owned, bars and dance clubs were very enjoyable to me. That's part of his legacy, but to be honest, I love taverns, bars and nightclubs!

Despite the alcohol and drug problems associated with them, I've met some absolutely wonderful people in those places. Dorothy's Club[2] can be found there!

Identity Theft

Throughout my early childhood, when I was looking to be affirmed and empowered as a male by my father and mother, one of my sisters, especially, often declared that I was a fag, a queer and a homo. I didn't even know what those words meant. My parents shouldn't have agreed and participated in the identity attacks, but many times they did and joined in the chorus. But that's a dysfunctional family. Excuses used to be made that many families were "dysfunctional" so it was justified. It seems to me that there were only a couple options. We could be the *Brady Bunch* with Marcia or *All In the Family* with Archie and Edith, but nothing in between. I couldn't comprehend just a normal, happy, healthy family. I was led to believe that there weren't any, except maybe Mormons. I later found out that many of them have their issues as well.

My dad became an alcoholic and nightly fights ensued between him and my mom. I would hear the screaming and my mom yelling out my name to come help. Being just a child, I was scared and felt totally helpless. Sometimes I would tremble in fear with my head under a pillow to block it out and then there were those times I would try to get between them to stop it.

Because of my trying to step in to stop the fighting, coupled with enjoying going to church, one of my dear sisters mockingly tagged me with name "priestly." I actually liked that nickname because there was something in me even as a child that believed in a loving God. I thought being a priest for God was the highest honor. She may have meant it to be cruel but she was actually prophesying my true calling. She was very perceptive.

---

2 Dorothy's Club is a developing resource website started by Angel Willson. You can find out more on page 200 and at www.dorothysclub.org.

The nickname "priestly" may have been in my unforesee-able future, but so were all the other names she labelled me with. When we were young we used to chant the lyrics "sticks and stones may break my bones, but words will never hurt me." As you get older you realize words hurt far worse than sticks or stones and carry great power. The words you speak carry the power to bring about destruction, death and curses, or your words can have the power to bring about encouragement, bless-ing and life. The mean and cruel words that were put on me as labels at home were used to destroy my identity as a normal boy. Without realizing it, I succumbed to the powerful word curses that were being declared over my life. The curses now (except the "priestly" one), have been broken and nullified!

Chapter 2

The Pigsty

Dorothy and the Pigsty

Dorothy is bored and isn't experiencing relational intimacy with family members. She is insecure and has no vision for her future except existing in the unenlightened culture she is currently experiencing. She starts walking on the edge of the pigsty.[1]

Angel on the Edge

My memory isn't totally clear, but around fourth grade I began noticing homosexual tendencies. Being called queer, fag and homo at home by my sister and having no other male role model, I became increasingly insecure and began to long for connection with true maleness.

As I stated in the previous chapter, my dad was emotionally and physically distant. He wanted me to enjoy sports like he did, but he wasn't willing to engage in these same sports with me. In fact, I began resenting sports altogether because I saw so many of my friends with their fathers engaging them and having a great time. In fact, I began to long for some way to feel intimate, important and wanted by a man. I wanted my dad to be that man. I began to realize over time that when the baby aspect wore off, there seemed to be no place for a son.

---

1 Dorothy's precarious walk and fall into the pigsty is depicted in the movie, *The Wizard of Oz*. LeRoy, M. (Producer), & Fleming, V. (Director). (1939). *The Wizard of Oz* [Motion picture]. USA: Metro-Goldwyn-Mayer (MGM).

Backrubs came into play at times during sleepovers with my friends. There were no homosexual intentions at first, but it fed a need in me more so than my friends. I had a much stronger need for male touch and bonding than they did. I would watch the interactions between my friends and their dads and wonder what was wrong with me that my dad didn't interact with me in that way. My friends' fathers really seemed to enjoy their sons and appeared to be so proud of them. I interpreted this in two ways. First, he didn't enjoy me because I wasn't his natural born son. Second, my family including my dad, apparently thought I was what they called me...a fag, a queer and a homo.

I needed male touch. Male affection. Male intimacy. Backrubs gave me something that I was lacking. It felt warm, accepting and tender.

Sexual role modeling in my home was having *Playgirl* soft porn magazines lying out in the open and a nude pin up of Burt Reynolds that a sister liked on a downstairs bathroom wall. I had to look at Burt Reynolds private parts every time I used that bathroom. No one was role modeling homosexual behaviors, but no one was role modeling proper sexual development either. I was taught in grade school from peers that in order to be a real male, you needed to hit every sexual base up to a "home run" with a girl to prove you weren't gay. I hit third base in grade school due to peer pressure which made me insecure with girls. Whether it was males or females, family culture or school culture, all of it was teaching me that moral boundaries were gray. There were unspoken rules that you had to hit all the sexual bases in order to be a "normal" American boy.

Since I was being called homosexual names at home before I ever experienced those things, there was constant anxiety inside of me. I felt I needed to prove that I wasn't what my family was telling me by doing the sexual bases with girls. I hated it all. It made me afraid but I had to survive. Sexual experiences, mostly with guys, gave me a sense of intimacy, belonging and bonding and helped me to survive emotional hell. Having different degrees of sex with females helped me to survive the psychological survival through heterosexual peer pressure. My needs in grade school weren't sexual. They were more emotional and psychological. That's what home was supposed to provide but it didn't. It didn't deliver the promise that I was chosen and accepted or that I was loved and celebrated. Instead I was criticized and felt tolerated. This ended in me being mentally and emotionally emasculated, and obliterated. I, as a person, died.

When the backrubs were happening my conscience was telling me I was liking it too much. I began to realize that it meant more to me than those who were doing it with me. I felt my needs were greater than theirs. This was me walking on the edge of the fence. It seemed a little risky at the time, but in no way did I think I would ever fall into the mud of sexual promiscuity and become morally wounded.

Falling Into the Mud

Those backrubs turned into touching of inappropriate places. Over time the same sexual bases came into play here as well. It wasn't until I was around 18 that I had my first homosexual "home-run." It came through a young man cruising me at an inner city park. I had been experiencing different levels of homosexuality by this time, but not the "home-run" level. He was very attractive to me and invited me to his home, introducing me to that level. A major boundary was broken in my conscience. I always believed in my mind that that level with a man was definitely a "forbidden pleasure."

Masturbation and oral sex with guys was where I fell off the edge of the fence and into the mud. Even though I knew it went against my conscience, it felt strangely good. It had its own soothing comfort and helped me escape the negative feelings of my turbulent home life. There was so much fighting, yelling, and different levels of domestic violence at home, that sexual experiences became like a drug helping me to relax and chill. I totally believe the gravitational pull towards men was due to my lack of male bonding with my father mixed with unfair labels that were put on me in my child Identity development years. This is my theory. And who knows, maybe there was some "genealogical disposition" in my DNA. That doesn't tell me that God made me that way, but that through generational lines, a tendency or orientation could be a vulnerability I was born with. And that is no sin.

I heard it said that sharks are drawn to bleeding fish. I relate this to people who bully. I was bullied at home which made me fearful, insecure and anxious; and school bullying became a reflection of my home life. At school, I truly believe the sharks could smell the bloody emotional turmoil and came in for the kill. My entire home and school life was all about learning the skills of emotional, psychological and physical survival. I'm now a happy Angel fish.

The more lost I felt the more I would systematically sink deeper into the mud of moral degradation. I felt unwanted and rejected both at home and at school. I was verbally attacked and humiliated in some way every day in both places till I graduated from high school. I couldn't wait to graduate and get the hell out of Spokane. I didn't know how close I was to kissing Kansas bye bye, through a magic rescue rainbow coming to me from heaven's love. I'm ahead of myself. That's a later chapter.

My mom had many wounds, heartaches and disappointments and her life wasn't easy. I remember when she disciplined me with the belt, it felt as though much of her own anger, rage and hatred was being taken out on me. I became the family target. It is what I learned in psychology class as the scapegoat. It is a role in a dysfunctional and alcoholic family where one person is demonized so others can excuse their own behaviors taking the attention off their own faults. Perhaps, I was the family's coping mechanism. I was also adopted, and the middle child.

Before I graduated from high school I felt so much shame I was literally physically bent over from hearing the words over and over again, "shame on you!" Mixing that with the name calling and my own developing dysfunctional and coping behaviors, I lost any and all self worth. I was alone and felt like a piece of trash who was going to hell anyway, which left me disheartened. I felt I had no value, worth, or importance and would never amount to anything. I gave up trying.

At the age of 18, in my senior year of high school, I came out of the closet that was created for me to which I became imprisoned, and announced to friends and family that I was gay. The mud of broken sexual boundaries, which still went against my conscience, became strangely comfortable. I got stuck and then I took occupancy. I thought this was as good as my life would ever get. Because of this I became an easy target for another kind of shark–a sexual predator. I was hanging out on the streets in a gay cruising area called "The Fruit Loop." (I remember being called a fruit as a child, so it seemed only natural that I ended up in the Loop). An older-young man, found and befriended me and began to groom me for male prostitution. Reminds me of the Artful Dodger in the story *Oliver Twist* who brought and groomed the lost street orphan, Oliver, into the community of runaway street orphans who made a living picking a pocket or two.

I hitchhiked from my "Kansas"–Spokane–through Seattle, where I stayed for six months. I then hitchhiked with three flaming gay queens after drugging for two nights at the gay chic Monastery Dance Club to the gay Castro District in San Francisco. Our hitchhiking journey from Seattle to San Francisco almost resembled the queers in the movie, *Priscilla, Queen of the Desert!* When I arrived in San Francisco and was dropped off, I met a German man. He took me home and introduced me to crystal meth and stuck a needle in my arm. He didn't do it by force. I already had experimented with other drugs in the Pigsty, so I was open to this new and harder one. He looked like a homo-erotic version of *Thomas of Finland*, the porn cartoon I had found somehow as a teenager. Pornography along with masturbation in my earlier teen and childhood days helped me escape the pain of life. It was like a tranquilizer. The images I viewed in pornography powerfully influenced me to want to seek out and find these fantasies and lose myself in them. Dorothy walked the fence, lost her balance and sank into the mud.

Nothing much mattered anymore except finding anything that would give me pleasure. The only thing that gave me pleasure was deeper forbidden pleasures. That was all I felt the world really offered me. I had no idea that God gave a crap about me and if He did care, why would He have made me so defective? Being given away by my birth mother and then treated so badly as "the chosen baby" at home cemented into my heart that I was damaged goods from the very beginning. There was no hope. I was lost.

I was beginning to learn the ways of male prostitution and be-coming stuck in the mud. I was turned on to other sexual bound-ary breakers such as porn shops, gay cruising parks, dark and trendy bathhouses, and other secret trysting places for homo-sexual connections. I also broke several drug boundaries.

Dorothy fell into the mud. So did I. Dorothy didn't get trampled by the pigs. I did. I was handed a death sentence. Through drug use and unsafe sex the consequences came to be. I was exposed to HIV-AIDS.

Chapter 3

Marvel

Dorothy's Experience With a Spiritual Counterfeit, Called a Professor

Dorothy believes she has to run away from home to save her heart from being destroyed and tells Toto they have to leave. Running away from home, Dorothy encounters a travelling fortune teller. He's not the real deal, but has a father's heart. In the movie he uses a crystal ball convincing Dorothy he has received information from the spirit world regarding what is happening back home.[1] Unbeknownst to Dorothy he sneaks information from her basket regarding her and Auntie Em. The Professor then acts as though Auntie Em is appearing to him in the crystal ball and tells her that she is so worried about losing Dorothy. He tells Dorothy that her Auntie Em could have a heart attack or die from a broken heart. He was kind with a father's heart, wanting to prod this lost orphan girl homeward where he thought she'd be safe. Later in the story, he appears as the fake Wizard who also developed a father's heart for Dorothy, again, trying to get her back home.

Dorothy had left home because she didn't feel safe. Her Toto-heart was under attack and she didn't feel her home environment was sound. She felt threatened, although she loved her Auntie Em.

I also ran away from home a few times. These were practice sessions for the time when I felt I could really get out of my "un-

---

1 Dorothy's encounter with Professor Marvel is depicted in the movie, *The Wizard of Oz*. LeRoy, M. (Producer), & Fleming, V. (Director). (1939). *The Wizard of Oz* [Motion picture]. USA: Metro-Goldwyn-Mayer (MGM).

safe" home environment. My heart had been attacked and damaged and I wanted out the moment I graduated from high school.

The Ouija Board Gets Me Back Home

I had a Ouija board. For some reason my family had one downstairs in the basement. One time I had a friend try it with me and
to my great and eerie surprise the plastic slider began to move on
its own, spelling out sentences. I always wanted to have spiritual
experiences. I had read some books on creative dreaming, astral
projection and things of that nature. None of them ever worked
for me. I never saw myself as a spiritual person but I was drawn
to mystical things since childhood. I loved doing magic and card
tricks. I loved magicians and I would do book reports on Houdini
and magic-oriented people like Walt Disney for school assign-
ments.

During one of my runaway excursions, the spirits channeling
through the Ouija board told me that my adoptive mother was
really my birth mother and that she had lied to me. After it told
me this I called my mom and asked her to meet me at a park.
She met me and had to spend at least an hour trying to convince
her poor lost child that it wasn't true. I finally believed her, because I could read her heart. Once, the board even told me that
it was Jesus Christ. I actually had a problem with that because it
had lied about my mother and I believed that Jesus never lied. It
caused me to wonder what kind of spirit was talking to me because this one was trying to deceive me. It also gave me another
name, which was interpreted as "Transparent Voyager."

I had a hard time in life trying to hold on to what I believed was
truth and love and I was weary of the battle. My heart was nearly
Toto-lly destroyed!

My poor mother! I had run away once again. Just like Dorothy,
the fortune teller's crystal ball caused her to come back home to
Auntie Em. I also returned home to my mom.

Chapter 4

Tornado Translation

*Who hath delivered us from the power of darkness,
and hath translated us into the power, authority, and
benevolent rule of God's Son...*

Colossians 1:1 (KJV)

As Dorothy is running back home, Auntie Em is desperately crying out for her because of a terrible wind storm. A large tornado is heading their way, a perfect storm in which they must seek safety and shelter in the storm cellar. Auntie Em is distraught as Dorothy is not among them. Unable to find her, Auntie Em, Dorothy, along with her little dog Toto, seeks shelter in her bedroom. She becomes unconscious in this swirling chaos. This is where she begins to experience a dream world, or is it?

The tornado picks up the house causing it to spin around, as a song by the pop group, Dead or Alive, sings, "You spin me round, round, round, like a record spinning round, round, round, round!" The name "Dead or Alive" is an appropriate title for the spinning round song!

Dorothy was translated from one world to another by a tornado. My life had also been the perfect storm. Similar to the prodigal son story that Jesus shared, the son ended up in the pigsty with the pigs. So did I as I shared in the last chapter. The prodigal son lost everything; his identity, his honor, his career, his reputation and his family. I will now share with you how the storm carried me to another spiritual reality.

Angel Meets Jesus at the West Hollywood Gay Pride Parade

In 1983, at the age of 19, I ended up in West Hollywood. A friend dropped me off by the gay prostitution strip called Boys Town located on Santa Monica Blvd. Now it's called WeHo. Hmmmm. Interesting. I now declare that it shall be called, We-Ho-ly! But I'm ahead of the story.

I was picked up by an audio producer who worked with major productions such as MTV, the academy, and music awards as well as various media productions. Living with him for about a month, I began to meet actors, singers and producers. I joined him while he did the audio production of Stevie Nicks "Stand Back" video on location and got to meet her. One evening, at a party with my friend in his condo outdoor patio, I was sitting poolside at a birthday party for one of the directors of the movie *Heaven Can Wait* when Mary Kay, the CEO of Mary Kay Cosmetics, came and sat with me. She was like an angel and a mother. She was very kind and just spent some time with me which I truly appreciated. I'm sure she knew that I was a lost gay child...a West Hollywood house boy. She touched my heart and I will never forget her.

The Gay Parade was happening during the month that I lived there. A girl I had known from my high school drama class had moved down to LA. We had been friends and we both really wanted to break into acting and media. We decided to meet. Little did she know she was in for a rude awakening and a culture shock when she joined me at the Gay Parade. That morning I was on a mix of hard drugs...crystal meth, LSD and half a quaalude. My poor friend had never seen me like this. I was functional but then again I wasn't. I had to wear dark glasses due to my eyes getting misaligned. The parade to me was like a rainbow tracer. We walked around and I wanted to show her what some gay bars were like. One of them was a leather bar. It was overwhelming for my friend and freaked her out. It was too much for her and she left early. It was a good thing she did!

I kept walking in my drug-induced daze for hours through the noisy and colorful rainbow crowd. As the day wore on the drugs began to wear off. My eyes came back to normal. Something strange began to happen and I wasn't sure if it was paranoia from the drugs or something real. I started noticing this brown car circling the blocks and passing me. This continued to happen for quite a while. I started to get nervous wondering if I was being watched or targeted. Being on the streets, using drugs and hooking up with strangers on the scene could certainly be cause for something like this to happen. For example, after receiving money from a "trick" I put it in my sock. A man with a chain in his hand began to follow me on the street. I started walking faster. He began to speak authoritatively for me to stop and for some reason it paralyzed me and I stopped. I didn't feel that I could run, so I turned and faced him asking what he wanted. He put the chain to my neck and told me to give him my money. He knew it was in my sock and forced me to hand it over. This happened in broad daylight in front of many pedestrians passing by! He got my money. This is what WeHo is like. It's scary, especially if you're a vulnerable gay teenager on the streets with no family or anyone who knows you or where you're from. It's very dangerous!

Back to the parade...as the day turned to night, this car kept circling and was not going away. I was really nervous. Having drugs in my system didn't help my fears. Sex traffickers find people like me and God only knows what they do.

I had had an experience with someone in the porn industry during that month. I was on very dangerous ground. I was wanting to go into normal movies like many people do who go to Hollywood to find their opportunity. I'm quite sure that if I had stuck around, I probably would have been scouted out and brought into the porn movie industry. That was not my goal but it could easily have been the goal of someone scouting me from the street. I never found out. Thank God!

My Father Who Art in Heaven

I didn't want to go home and possibly put my friend in danger. So I kept walking. I started walking up Santa Monica Boulevard towards Beverly Hills.

As I was walking, I think at about two in the morning, strong thoughts came to me about God and Jesus. I was so afraid by this time that I was shaking. All I could think of at this point was death, heaven and hell. I began to have an awareness like never before that I was standing at a spiritual threshold. I was so scared I actually went to a police officer for help. I didn't mind going to jail at this point in order to get off the streets and to be safe. The cop said he couldn't help me because he was busy with someone else. The parade was long over and I seemed to be the last to leave. I was alone and then I began to be aware of some kind of a communication from above, but it was coming from within me. It was an internal dialogue that I knew wasn't my doing. It was God. He said to me, "You're standing at a door of choice. I want you to choose to give Me your life." I had believed in Jesus my entire life and wanted Him, but I couldn't change. I didn't think it was possible that I could be a Christian. At that moment I even told God that I wanted to give Him my life but I was unable to change. I told him that I was gay. Once again that internal dialogue spoke, saying "I'm not asking you to change." That statement took me aback and I wondered what He meant. Did He mean I could be a gay Christian? That would be a relief but I never heard teachers of the Bible say that you could be both. God then explained it better by saying "I'm not asking you to change. I'm asking you to surrender! Put your trust in Me and follow Me." That was beyond change and even transcended change. He was telling me to let go and to let God. It wasn't a Bible or a church that was speaking to me. It was God Himself, and even though I had done drugs many hours earlier, this was not the drugs, this was very real. I wasn't out of my mind. In fact, I was quite coherent.

I began to shake and tremble even more. To me, this was almost scarier than the thought that I was being followed by someone who wanted to kidnap or kill me. And yet, it was like a door of hope had just opened. I knew who Jesus was. I grew up in America. I went to churches at times and heard the gospel message every Christmas and Easter. I always liked what Jesus represented and who He was portrayed to be. He was the one who was tenderly holding the little sheep and children in His arms in the pictures on my kindergarten classroom wall. I dreamed of Him holding me in His arms as well.

I was wearing a black leather jacket that I had purchased in the gay Castro District of San Francisco. I became gravely aware that my life wasn't right with God and I had a multitude of sins against me. I couldn't claim rights to heaven. I was a good person and had a good heart, as my Grandmother Nan would testify about me, but I was a sinner. It wasn't just homosexuality, promiscuity, drugs and prostitution, which were the more obvious sins, but the independent spirit I had chosen where I would always choose to do things my way and not God's way. My way was bringing death and destruction. God's way would bring me a new life, hope, healing and a future.

It was now a choice of life or death—spiritually as well as physically.

I did something that I had never done, nor had I ever seen. No one had ever done this in any church I'd been to, although today most everyone does it in churches that have the Holy Spirit's true presence being felt. I raised my hands to heaven. I didn't think of it as putting your hands up in surrender to one more powerful, but that's what I was doing. Tears of joy and fear were in my eyes. I was shaking. I began to speak out loud. I didn't know how to pray. The only prayer I knew was the Lord's Prayer. I never believed God heard my prayers. Prayer to me was just reciting things in a spiritually dead church like the Lord's Prayer. Jesus called it vain repetitions which he told his believers to not practice. To me, prayer was always one-sided. There was no God listening or responding to me. Prayers were vain to me. I wondered why I should waste my time reciting prayers in church buildings when God was only on the stained glass windows, the cross around the clergy's neck or the tiny crackers and thimbles of grape juice on the altar?

But this time I was getting a communication...a heavenly phone call. A call was being put upon my life. I began to pray the Lord's Prayer line by line. Instead of just reciting it like I always had in the past, I began to think of the meaning of the words and pray them out loud in a personal kind of way. Instead of saying, "Our Father," I said "My Father." I never felt I had a father. Here I was now, addressing God as my personal father and me as His personal son. This was a paradigm shift. I went on through the prayer, "forgive me my sins...keep me from temptation and deliver me from evil... for Thine is the kingdom, the power and the honor forever."

I took off my leather Castro jacket and dropped it to the ground, leaving it behind. It was black and to me was representing my sins, meaning everything that was against God's way and plan for my life. I began to walk forward towards Beverly Hills in the middle of Santa Monica Boulevard praying out loud with my hands up in the air. There's a great song I heard in the gay bars with the lyrics, "Put your hands up in the air, put your hands up in the air!" I did what they said!

Then out of the depths of my being vows came to my mind. These were not New Year's resolutions! I felt as though I was in some court with a judge. I felt my words were being recorded and weighed. I had to say what I meant and mean what I said. I began to tell God that if He would save me I would give him my entire life, forever.

The second vow was that if He wanted me to join a monastery to be wholly His, I would. I couldn't believe I said that! What was I thinking? God later held me to that, but taught me how to host His divine presence within my heart.

The third vow was that no matter how hard it would be for me, I would never give up. This last vow was really important for me to make because I knew myself very well. In my own mind I knew there was no way I could ever live up to all this. I knew how weak and frail I was. I couldn't imagine a lifetime of being a boring Sunday church going Christian or becoming a religious monk in a monastery. Both of those sounded extremely boring to the point of feeling like death to me. That's why Jesus spoke to my heart and said to trust and follow Him because He was going to bring me into a heavenly experience and lifestyle that I never dreamed of. He had a rainbow surprise for me!

Suddenly it was as if a gentle spiritual breeze flowed through me and around me. A tranquility happened. Everything, within and without, became very still and serene. The drug effect, the fear and all anxiety was turned into serenity. I then realized that a transaction had just happened between God and me. I didn't understand the technicalities of it all but I knew at that moment my life would never be the same. There is a scripture that says, "If a man be in Christ, he has become a new creation, old things have passed away. Behold, all things have become new." -2 Corinthians 5:17

Angel Becomes a Hollywood Star

Like many people, I wanted and needed others to see me as someone special. I thought becoming a star in Hollywood would be a sure ticket for that. That dream never happened. Years later the Lord spoke to my heart and said, "You actually became a star in Hollywood. You didn't become a world's star, you became God's star. You are a shining one that gives hope and direction to many."

*Do everything without grumbling or arguing, so that
you may become blameless and pure, "children
of God without fault in a warped and crooked
generation." Then you will shine among them like
stars in the sky as you hold firmly to the word of life.*

Philippians 2:14-16 NIV

Chapter 5

The LGBT Rainbow

Seven is the New Six!

Gilbert Baker holds two world records for the largest flag. The first is for the rainbow flag he made in 1994 to commemorate the 25th anniversary of the Stonewall Riots. This is when the LGBT community stood up to abusive police in Greenwich Village in New York City. It made history and things changed. The second is for the rainbow flag he made in 2003 commemorating the 25th anniversary of the original Rainbow flag he created in 1978.

Just recently as of writing this book, Gilbert Baker passed away. It's a new day for a renewed rainbow. The rainbow that Gilbert created contained six beautiful colors and each had its own meaning. In the Bible, the number six is the number for humanity. God's original rainbow has seven colors. Seven is the number of completion.

I am proclaiming a new day for LGBTQ. A color called Indigo is part of God's original rainbow that is presently in the sky after storms and the rain. Indigo, again according to *The Rainbow God* by Johnny Enlow, represents "divine revelation." A new spiritual revelation of the heavenly Father will open up a fresh relationship with heavens love and power, through faith in Jesus. This will result in personal identity revelations as the color indigo is honored as one of God's colors for you.

I had many identity names placed on me as a child, such as fag, queer, and homo. Jesus took away the old person, with its old identities and transformed me into what He says I am.

Jesus saves us from wrath and judgment. In Him there is no condemnation when we receive His free gift of salvation. As we receive Him as Savior and confess Him as Lord of our life He becomes the completed rainbow in us and is transforming us into "Reign-bow" saints. The book of Romans says that through the gift of righteousness that Jesus became in our place, and the abundance of divine enablement, called grace, we reign as Kings in life—Reign-bow Kings and Queens! We become part of His Imperial Courts. This show is not a drag!

Keep ahold of your rainbow and don't let go! God is thrusting it into a new dimension. Don't be satisfied with only six colors, which was important in its day, but lay hold of your rightful inheritance. The seventh color completes us and turns and transforms LGBT into L.overs of G.od B.eing T.rue! I am a completed LGBT. Seven is the new six!

News Update

As I am finishing this book, getting ready to publish it in a couple of days, the news came to me that the LGBTQ community has now added two more colors...black and brown, to represent honoring people of color being included in the community. This now makes an eight colored rainbow. Eight is God's number of new beginnings. This is prophetic because as I have written, it's a new day for the LGBTQ community. God's love is ready to be poured out upon all the community, to every color!

Chapter 6

Witch in the Window

*Our battle is not against people, but against
witchcraft, and evil forces of wickedness in the air.*

Ephesians 6:12

As Dorothy's house was spinning in the whirlwind, she wakes from her concussion and peers out the window.[1] She sees her cruel neighbor who hated Toto and watches her shapeshift into a wicked witch. It was just like Dorothy had thought! Fear once again engulfs Dorothy even between these two worlds. It seemingly follows her everywhere. For the first time Dorothy is beginning to learn spiritual realities that were behind all of the bullying and attacks that came against her. I will share in another chapter about finding my birth mother. I discovered that she was being pressured by her father to have an abortion for convenience. She didn't buckle under his personal agenda. I was targeted for death and destruction even before I was born.

> *Oh yes, you shaped me first inside, then out;*
> *you formed me in my mother's womb.*
> *I thank you, High God—you're breathtaking!*

---

1 Dorothy's flight and arrival at Oz, chronicled in the book, is visually depicted in the movie. LeRoy, M. (Producer), & Fleming, V. (Director). (1939). *The Wizard of Oz* [Motion picture]. USA: Metro-Goldwyn-Mayer (MGM).

Body and soul, I am marvelously made!
I worship in adoration–what a creation!
You know me inside and out,
you know every bone in my body;
You know exactly how I was made, bit by bit,
how I was sculpted from nothing into something.
Like an open book,
you watched me grow from conception to birth;
all the stages of my life were spread out before you,
The days of my life all prepared
before I'd even lived one day.

Psalm 139: 13-17 (Message Bible)

Evil in the Rainbow

Dorothy notices something in her transition from one realm to another. She is being followed by an evil entity, seeing it outside her window as she is swirling around in the tornado.

After my encounter with God at the Gay Pride Parade something scary and threatening happened the next day. I was not high or affected in the least by any drug I had taken from the previous morning. I was to discover again that my God experience was very real and not an illusion or some paranoid effect from any drug. My tornado transition wasn't a dream. It was real. But it also seemed like a dream because it was all so strange and surreal. It was like a whirlwind in my mind.

Kidnapped!

I had met a lady at the parade who had given me a Christian leaflet along with her phone number. I called her the next morning. When she answered the phone I told her about the experience I had had with God the previous night. She asked if I'd like to go to a church service with her and she would happily pick me up. I agreed. She picked me up taking me to some church building in a seedy part of West Hollywood. Taking our seats and hearing some man behind a podium speaking, I began to feel something wasn't right. In fact, I had this growing sense that my life was in danger. I had never felt anything like this, even though I had been in harm's way many times before. Nothing was happening that revealed any danger except for the shady people standing around the church building on the street corners.

After the service it was time to go. I actually felt like leaving without telling this lady but she wouldn't leave my side. She introduced me to a couple of her friends and told me they would be joining us in the car to take me home.

I didn't live very far away and was told they would take me right home. As she drove past my place of residence, I mentioned she had just missed the turn. She reassured me they were taking me home but the sense of danger I was feeling kept growing, especially when she started driving through downtown Los Angeles. I asked if I could call a friend of mine and surprisingly she agreed. Stopping at a phone booth I intuitively began to think about a strategy to get away. As I picked up the phone another car suddenly pulled up and a man got out, picking up the phone next to me but he wasn't pressing any numbers or talking. I felt that somehow this man was connected to these people and I was possibly being set up for something bad.

I called my friend, who answered. She was quite confused about my one-sided conversation. It was obvious this man next to me was listening to my phone call. Telling these people my friend was waiting for me, they assured me they would take me there right away but continued to drive in the opposite direction. It was now evening and getting dark.

Something was terribly wrong and I began to become aware that I was being kidnapped! This represents the wicked witch passing Dorothy's window threatening her on her journey over the rainbow.

Back in the car I began to pray quietly and desperately to God. I told Him that if He would save me from this situation I'd completely give my life to Him as I had vowed the night before at the parade. I repeated the same vows and reaffirmed my choice and commitment to live for Him, His way, for the rest of my life.

Religion Couldn't Save Me

I just had to roll with these scary people for the time being and see what would happen. I was totally dependent upon this personal God. No religion could have helped me in this situation. It was going to have to be another direct God experience similar to the one I had the night before. I would soon find out if God was really with me or not, or if that was just some false spiritual experience I had from drug effects altering my mind.

God, Save the Queen!

Suddenly a new strategy came to my mind. Although they didn't tell me they were kidnapping me, I'm sure they knew that I knew something was amiss. It didn't take a rocket scientist to figure it out. I told them I was thirsty and wanted to stop at a convenience store to get something to drink. They consented and stopped at one nearby. I went in and instead of buying anything to drink I just stood at the counter under the surveillance camera. I didn't leave. One of the men from the car came in and told me we needed to go. I told him I was just fine and was going to stay there and they were free to go. He left and then the lady came in and said to get in the car and they would take me home. I refused and then I looked at the clerk behind the counter asking him for help because I felt my life was in danger from these people. He backed away not wanting to get involved. The man didn't even call the police.

I was still holding on to the God of yesterday. I told the lady I wasn't going with them. I was trapped and didn't feel that I could run. She then, forcefully ordered me into the car but I stood my ground. At this point it was obvious I was being kidnapped. She walked out the door and they waited in the car which was parked right outside the front door. I couldn't stay in the store all night so I took a deep breath and said, "God, do something. I belong to You now. I am in Your hands."

I walked slowly outside in front of their car and raised my hands to heaven just as I had done the night before at the parade. I looked up to heaven and began to pray The Lord's Prayer out loud again. I just began to walk in the dark, afraid of being captured, fearing for my life, fearing God. I walked right past them! I didn't look back, I just kept walking. It was as if I walked right through them and a magic cloak had been placed over me to hide me.

I don't know how far I walked but it seemed forever. I saw a restaurant with a police officer standing in the parking lot. I asked him if he'd watch over me while I made a phone call to my friend to come pick me up. I told him I was in danger and didn't know if someone was following me. He did.

When my friend picked me up at this restaurant, he told me it was most likely a cult that had tried to kidnap me and I should leave Hollywood and go back home. He knew that I was too young and vulnerable to the dangers of Hollyweird. He was trying to help me. I agreed and left within a few days.

My Heavenly Father Who Art on Earth!

I didn't know what it was like to actually have an engaged father in my life. When I called out to God both nights, I called him, "My Father, Who art in heaven," as I had learned as a child. Just because someone has the name dad or father in your life doesn't always mean they are one. I had to courageously decide to give God a chance after I had been let down for so many years by my adopted father. If my father didn't engage with me as his "chosen baby" then why would the Father, Who art in heaven? This fulfilled a scripture from Psalm 119:170...

May my prayer come before You; deliver me according
to Your promise.

God allowed me to experience the attempted kidnapping so I would call upon Him and, once again, see how He would answer me. He was showing me that my encounter with Him at the parade was not a drug experience but was one that was real and true. I would begin to discover that a relationship was developing between us...one of a Father and a son.

Chapter 7

Munchkin Community

Dorothy's Kansas, as described in *The Wonderful Wizard of Oz*, was grim.[1] When she looked out "she could see nothing but the great gray prairie on every side." When she first reaches Oz in contrast, Dorothy gives a "cry of amazement" as she is struck by the land's "marvelous beauty." It took a storm of life and a little heart named Toto to get to this new realm which looks like a prayer sung long ago. It was something about another place where troubles melt and bluebirds sing. It had to be somewhere over a seven colored rainbow.

Dorothy, with Toto in her arms, opens the door of her house which represents her soul to this new realm. It's a different kingdom filled with technicolor hues of incredible light. Her every sense is in total awe as she walks through the exotic flowers, the singing diamond water and the dreamy bluebirds flying in this intoxicating atmosphere.

Dorothy begins to hear a heavenly song coming out of everything she is seeing. Everything created seemed to have an aura of splendor in it and coming through it. There were heavenly bluebirds singing a new song. Love was in the air like she had never felt before and she could hear laughter. There was a divine peace

---

1 Baum, L. Frank. *The Wonderful Wizard of Oz*. The Project Gutenberg EBook. 1900. Web. <http://www.gutenberg.org/files/55/55-h/55-h.htm>.

in this atmosphere. It looked and felt like joy, grace and kindness. It was so beautiful and welcoming. Nothing smelled like religion. It was true spirituality. It was like being a newborn baby discovering a marvellous new world.

I returned home to Spokane after my attempted kidnapping. Everything around me seemed to have a spiritual technicolor hue to it. It was so very strange. I had never heard birds sing so beautifully. Creation seemed alive and personal. I was now experiencing everything, not just from my own senses, but from an awakened spiritual sense in me that was in union with God, who was now in me. I didn't understand this new vision at all but I knew it had to do with my surrender to Christ. I learned soon after that God's very spirit, His essence had been deposited in me. I was no longer just a human but a heavenly man. Dorothy didn't realize this until something was placed on her feet.

After returning to Spokane, I searched for a Christian friend of mine whom I had met when I was 18. From day one this man had always treated me with respect and dignity. He loved Jesus and shared about Him to many people, and his wonderful treatment of me inspired my interest toward Jesus. Reconnecting with him, I told him about my story in West Hollywood. He was very happy for me and began to help me learn more about God.

Munchkins - My First Spiritual Community

I was praying with a gay friend of mine who wanted the Jesus I experienced at the parade. Praying together, he accepted Jesus into his heart. We both began to hear an open air Christian preacher in the park. We were excited to go meet him and maybe find some people who could help mentor us in our new Christian journey. As we approached him, we asked if they had a church meeting where we could visit. They invited us to a Wednesday night meeting and we went. I could really feel God's presence and peace in this meeting. I felt so much joy I could hardly contain myself because God's spirit in me was alive and I felt new and vibrant. I felt as though I was in heaven.

I discovered they had a house where Christian brothers lived together as part of this spiritual community. I'm going to call them Munchkins. I wanted to live with these brothers and asked if I could live there because I desired to live fully for God's will and purpose for my life. After talking together they agreed, but only if I got a job to pay my share of the rent.

I moved in and became part of this new spiritual community. I would later learn they were spiritually dwarfed by leaders who were authoritarian and controlling, causing them to be spiritually stunted in their growth.

It was something akin, in the movie version, to what the Munchkins called the Lollipop Guild. They may have been dwarfed, but they acted very happy and loved to sing songs and praises to God in their limited, controlled heavenly realm.

Beat the Gay Away!

Despite the fact that these Munchkins were Spirit-filled and were part of the Kingdom of God, they had issues. They were under the witch's control of fear-based religion. When I joined this community, I developed an accountability relationship with one of the elders. When I would slip into some sexual former behavior, I would confess it with tears. It was very humiliating for me to talk about my struggles with someone who had never experienced the gay sexual culture. I felt like a square peg in a round hole. It was embarrassing, but I felt I had to be in the light for the sake of my conscience before God. I discovered that when I would indulge in my carnal desires I would lose the sweet fellowship of God's spirit. It was horrible. Sin became more painful to me, because I was experiencing such a deep tranquil presence of God within me. When I did things that were against what was right, I would feel a painful burning in place of the peaceful joy. I was realizing that the Holy Spirit in me was actually a person and not just an energy or force. I could actually grieve the heart of God's spirit. The Bible says to confess your faults and sins to one another so we can have fellowship with God and each other. I could feel the absence of God when I indulged. You see, I had developed sexual addiction, so it wasn't easy for me to shape up right away, due to my unrenewed mind. I still believed I was the old me, even though I had become a New Creation saint in Jesus Christ. There is a process, and it's tailor-made for each of us in our developing relationship with God.

After six months of struggling and being completely honest with the elders, trying with all my heart to overcome the power of my past conditioning, I was verbally and publicly cast out of the congregation on a Sunday morning so that I'd repent. I walked out feeling awful from the humiliating rejection. I fell back into my past gay identity and sexual behaviors and ended up back on the streets of Seattle and San Francisco. I was cast out despite my struggles and my honesty. I was only six months old in Christ...a spiritual baby.

A year and a half later, while in San Francisco, I began to really miss my relationship with God. I had fallen asleep in the poppies. I was lost again, and didn't know if there was hope for me. I began to feel afraid for my life and flew back home to my home church. I told them in great tears that I was sorry for my sins and that I was ready to give it all to God. They kept me in isolation for a month and wouldn't let me go to their church or to any others. During that month I was tormented with fear. I would sweat and shake in bed. I thought that if my church denied me then I would surely go to hell and it would be worse than if I had never been saved. After a month, they let me return. I was told to confess my embarrassing sexual sins publicly to the congregation. It was beyond humiliating. I was shaking with great fear and tears were flowing. After I publicly confessed sexual sins, the elder had me lay down on the floor on Sunday morning. He instructed a mother and father figure they had appointed for my personal growth and wholeness, to beat me with a board in front of the congregation as "fatherly discipline." They said it was because I was never disciplined by a father at home. So this public humiliation was going to heal me. They tried to beat the gay out of me. Jesus actually took the beating which made me a new creation 2000 years ago. People call it "the finished work of the cross."

I was being vulnerable and courageous. I was willing to suffer extreme humiliation before men that I would be accepted by God. I wanted God's love and favor above anything and I would have let them beat the crap out of me, if that's what God wanted. But that's what religion does. God doesn't torment, humiliate and abuse his children who are honestly trying to please their heavenly Father.

Soon after, I began to realize that something was desperately wrong with this group. Knowing them, I knew many of them really loved the Lord, but they were under the religious witch's power. They were Munchkins...undeveloped and controlled by authoritarian fear-based Wizards.

I left that place and found a church that was a like a green pasture which restored my soul. They welcomed me and loved me to wholeness throughout the years.

Jesus saved me from some of His followers and led me to others who would nurture my soul and help me develop out of munchkin-hood to spiritual adulthood. In *The Wonderful Wizard of Oz* book and story, the Munchkins were under the power and control of the witch. The book of Galatians in the New Testament equates religion based on performance as witchcraft (Galatians 3:1-5). For it is by God's grace we are saved through faith in Him. It is not performance based. My journey in the kingdom of God taught me how to separate the good, the bad and the ugly. I have learned not to throw the baby out with the bath water. I didn't reject all Christians because of the wounds, abuses and offenses I received from those who didn't understand the heavenly Father's true heart of love.

Chapter 8

What Kind of Witch are You?

Welcome to the Supernatural Community

As Dorothy encounters the Munchkins in the new land of Oz, a rainbow-hued bubble comes down from the heavens and lands in front of Dorothy.[1] It is Glinda, who I am representing as the Holy Spirit, who is the voice of God. She is absolutely divine! Asking Dorothy what kind of witch she is, she points to the house which had fallen on the Wicked Witch of the East, killing her. No one was ever able to defeat that witch and they were anxious to discover who this girl was who had fallen from the sky!

Dorothy Receives the Indwelling Holy Spirit

The house falling on the witch represents Jesus defeating satan's authority over the world through His death and resurrection on the cross. Dorothy came out of the house that destroyed satan's power when she received Christ and found herself "over the rainbow."

I had never experienced the power of God before. It wasn't until I returned home to Spokane that I found my friend who then introduced me to the Holy Spirit. He shared scriptures with me from the New Testament about how people could receive the

---

1 Dorothy has an initial encounter with the witch in the movie (LeRoy & Fleming, 1939) and the book (Frank Baum 1900) though the details vary.

Holy Spirit as another experience after receiving Christ. It reads that as Peter, one of Jesus' special messengers, was preaching, the Holy Spirit came upon everyone that was in the room and they began to speak in other languages, which the Bible calls tongues.

The gift of tongues is one of the powers that believers can receive after saying yes to Jesus as Savior and Lord. It's a spiritual heavenly language that you can pray at anytime, if you want, either quietly or out loud. It's a gift that helps you hear God's thoughts in your mind and opens up heavenly encounters. It will also activate other spiritual powers and gifts.

While my friend Chris prayed for me by laying his hand upon my head, I felt something rising in my throat. He was aware of what was happening and told me not to try to understand but to just open my mouth and release any sounds that would begin to come out. I felt weird but I knew something was happening. Sure enough, when I began to let the syllables out, they started coming out faster and faster. A different language was flowing out of my mouth. I had just received my first supernatural gift from the Holy Spirit.

I was beginning to discover through my friend that I was truly a child of God and I was being favored by God to know Him. Glinda, the Holy Spirit, was now in me as a close friend and comforter and I was now being guided on my journey for God's kingdom purposes.

Spiritual Guidance to a Gay Party

I travelled in sales with a publishing company selling advertising throughout the northwest. While I was in a town in Montana, I noticed some kind of LGBT group in a park. I had an hour until my next appointment so I decided to go and meet some new friends. I walked over introducing myself and we had a great conversation. They invited me to a party and wanted to introduce me to some friends from the gay community. I accepted their offer.

It was after work and as I was driving there I did not feel God's peace. I began to feel very anxious and didn't want to go to this party feeling this way but I felt in my heart that Glinda, the Holy Spirit, was guiding me to go and befriend them. Suddenly a truck pulled in front of me going really slow and the license plate had the words El Shaddai! This is one of God's Hebrew names. It means almighty and comforter. As I was reading the words El Shaddai on this license plate, suddenly a rush of divine peace came down on my head and filled me with such euphoric love and power.

Jesus, Glinda and I all went to the gay party! I walked into a room of strangers but new friends were waiting to happen. I was sent by God to bring heaven's love. His light that was shining through me gave me complete favor with everyone. We all became friends and because of my job selling restaurant advertising, I was able to treat them to dinners at wonderful restaurants.

A Gay Witch Gets Over the Rainbow

Glinda came through me by the guidance and love of the Holy Spirit, as El Shaddai, the divine comforter, friend and helper. I went to that town for three years in a row. I developed relationships with many of them over time and many wonderful things happened.

On one of my trips there I met a gay young man who told me he was a Wiccan. I didn't share my faith with him for three years. We just hung out and went for walks. The third year I felt that familiar impression to call and ask if I could come visit him. He agreed and informed me he wasn't feeling well. He was very sick and I don't recall what his sickness was. After our conversation, I felt I needed to share with him about my parade encounter with God. Because we had become true friends and I had listened to him many times, he trusted me and was all ears to hear my story. I began to share my testimony with him of getting "over the rainbow" through Jesus. I explained how it happened and some things God had done supernaturally in my life, which were incredible. He didn't reject it because he knew in his heart that I really was his friend and cared for him. He was really moved and inspired by what I had told him and I invited him to pray with me to receive Jesus. He agreed. As he asked Jesus into his heart, tears began to roll down his cheeks through his closed eyes. He responded that he could actually feel God was with him and could feel the peace of God's love and forgiveness. El Shaddai brought comfort and peace to his heart through his new found faith in what Jesus did for him. It was very touching and beautiful.

The next day at a thrift store I overheard two young gay men talking about a friend who had suddenly passed away the night before. I couldn't help but wonder if it was my friend. I approached them, introducing myself and asked who this person was they were talking about. I was shocked to discover that it was my friend, and shared with them about the experience we had a few hours before he died. They were surprised. I asked them if they could help me get in contact with his parents, which they did. I got to meet his parents and told them the story. His parents were extremely sad about the loss of their son but were very happy to hear about our friendship and what had transpired just before his death.

El Shaddai sent me to him to help him get "over the rainbow" just before he died. He is now in heaven with his Savior and Lord and is now an eternal L.over of G.od B.eing T.rue.

Dorothy began to discover that she was not a witch at all. But because of the "slippers" she was realizing a new supernatural lifestyle was guiding and using her to bring God's forgiveness, love and peace to LGBT.

Chapter 9

Glinda the Good Witch

New Orientation

Glinda, who represents God, the Holy Spirit guide, begins to reveal and explain to Dorothy about spiritual identities. She becomes Dorothy's interpreter helping her to understand the spiritual reality of good and evil entities at work behind the scenes. She makes Dorothy a new saint by giving her the "ruby slippers" that the Witch of the East was wearing before Dorothy's house killed her. In the original book, the slippers were silver. In the movie they are ruby. Silver represents the salvation and redemption found in Jesus Christ and ruby represents the shed blood of Christ that justifies us before God, meaning just as if we had never sinned. This qualifies us to receive the gift of the indwelling Holy Spirit along with all His powers. Because of the slippers, she is now fitting into a new identity with godly power. She is a baby in the spirit with no understanding but will grow up in Christ into a fully matured woman of God. Dorothy needs Glinda for her journey because she will re-orient, guide and reveal to her where she's going, how to get there and who she is as a new creation. In the book, Glinda kisses Dorothy and the imprint of that kiss remains on Dorothy. The kiss represents the union with God and all of God's protection against the evil one.

Glinda, metaphorically speaking, in this scene also represents the spirit of wisdom. The book of Proverbs depicts wisdom as a beautiful, gracious mother that instructs, guides and reveals. In the New Testament, Paul prayed for the followers of Jesus that they would receive the spirit of wisdom and revelation to know God better and to understand who they were in Christ. Remember that revelation to know God is represented as the color Indigo which is the seventh color of the Rainbow. In the story Glinda came down to Dorothy in a seven colored rainbow from heaven (bubble).

Dorothy, now adopted into a new spiritual family, is being asked by Glinda who she is as a spiritual person. Is she a good witch or a bad witch? Now on a learning curve, Dorothy is discovering her new identity and new names in this new realm. By receiving the spiritual gift of tongues, she also received a heavenly language. She was acclimating to a new spirituality from her Kansas identity as a powerless orphan to the Oz identity of adoption as an inheritor, not as inferior, but as one with spiritual authority.

At home in Kansas I had been called identity names such as fag, queer and homo. Now I was learning a new culture, a new identity, a new language and new behaviors, all of which were developing on my new journey. I was gay but now I was being called a saint. I was a caterpillar but was now a butterfly. I went from curses to affirmations. My orientation was changing because I was now born from a different womb carrying a different spiritual DNA. It was the DNA of God Himself.

The Gift of Prophecy

The first church I attended after my rainbow ride had ministries operating in spiritual gifts. Two of these gifts are called words of knowledge and prophecy. Words of knowledge are pieces of information about a person's past and prophecy is about a person's future. My first experience at this church was a guest speaker who spoke a prophetic word over me. He said that I would later be called to America as one who would hear God and help people to know Him for themselves on an experiential level. He had a title for it, but I prefer to explain what he meant instead. That was something I had never heard before or even thought about. It was a 180 degree paradigm shift.

I discovered that because of having the indwelling Holy Spirit, the slippers of God, that every child of God could prophesy. In 1 Corinthians 12 it says to eagerly desire the gift of prophecy above all other spiritual gifts because it builds people up, encourages and strengthens them. I was finding myself in a new family culture that had an ability to see each other and to see me through God's heart and to vocally affirm what God says about each of us. This new kingdom family was under God's command to build each other up, not tear each other down.

True followers of Jesus didn't call me a fag, a homo and a queer. They began to call me what God was revealing to them, not only who I presently was, but who I would become in my future. Without the Holy Spirit revealing to people who I was in Christ, I wouldn't have stood a chance to come out of what I had formerly thought of myself in my low self worth. In my experience, many Christians in the early 80's had a hard time believing gays, especially those with HIV, could be saved and baptized in the Holy Spirit and transformed into Christlikeness.

God was telling me that I would be a new kind of LGBT, a L.over of G.od B.eing T.rue. I found myself in a new family that affirmed and accepted me more than I had been accustomed to. Throughout the years I have received hundreds of prophetic words from traveling ministers and from the family of God. These spiritual gifts helped to shape my spiritual identity and ministry in a powerful way. I am no longer a queer. I'm a peculiar person. I'm no longer an ain't. I'm a saint. I'm no longer homo-genized, I'm pastor-ized!

Two Prophecies

On two different occasions that transpired many years apart, two guest speakers, without knowing me or my story, told me that I would be called by God to bring a message of love and demonstrations of God's heavenly power to the LGBT community. This is why I had to follow the Yellow Brick Road of revelation and transformation. I was called to become a special messenger to those who were singing this song:

If you believe in heaven above, do you believe in love...
send me an angel, right now...
sung by Real Life.

The LGBT community sang and danced to this prayer whenever I was in a gay bar or a dance club. Not realizing it at the time, God heard and was answering that prayer that we were all singing and dancing to. It's one thing to pray, "send me an angel" and it's another thing for God to raise one up to actually send! ...Especially one of their own. The word "angel" doesn't always mean a spiritual being in heaven, but can be a human messenger with a heavenly gift.

Chapter 10

Ruby Slippers

Stay inside of them. Their magic must be very powerful or she wouldn't want them so badly...

*- Glinda the Good Witch of the North
from the movie, The Wizard of Oz[1]*

The supernatural slippers represent our authority and power in releasing heaven on earth. I want LGBT people to see the supernatural slippers on their feet through Christ.

The house has landed on the Wicked Witch of the East, killing her. This is representative of Jesus' triumph over satan's power due to Adam and Eve's original sin which brought death and disorder into the world. The evil witch's sister, the Wicked Witch of the West, uses her powers of deception to rob Dorothy of her worth, identity and authority she has while wearing these slippers and demands that she hand them over. Satan and his demons, through fear, masquerading as religion, are always scheming and plotting to undermine your identity and power in the kingdom of God. The witch can't take it away but can only deceive you to not know who you are in your powerful new creation identity.

When we receive Christ, God deposits an anointing in you which carries great power. In John 1:1 it says that you have received an inner anointing from God. This anointing is represented by the God given slippers. It's your new spiritual DNA, containing all wisdom and power to accomplish your destiny. The Bible says that Christ in you is supernatural wisdom and power.

---

1 (LeRoy & Fleming, 1939)

Glinda tells Dorothy to keep her feet firmly planted inside these slippers and reminds her of the great power they carry. Why else would the witch want them so badly?

The only way for satan to take you out of your position in God is for you to choose to give it up. The Yellow Brick Road journey is about fighting the good fight of faith. Our battle, the scriptures say, is not actually with people but with spiritual forces of darkness. When you receive Christ and what the Bible calls the "indwelling of the Holy Spirit," the ruby slippers are placed on your feet. The seal of your inheritance is the Father's promise of the indwelling Holy Spirit, the anointing, for every L.over of G.od B.eing T.rue...the saints!

I was so enthralled with my new vision of the heavenly kingdom of God that I couldn't help but share my experiences of the reality of Jesus. I told family members, friends, anyone who would listen! Many people just laughed at me and said I was becoming a religious fanatic. My story was very real. The fact that my guilt was gone and replaced with divine peace meant that anyone who would respond with an open heart and a simple prayer could receive Jesus as their Savior and Lord. They could even receive the gift of the Holy Spirit.

There were not many people who wanted to pray with me to receive Jesus. It didn't stop me, but I was getting discouraged. I needed some backup from God and His power to do something supernatural! Jesus, being God personified and perfect love, said there were many people who wouldn't believe in Him unless He did miracles. Love was not enough. Jesus needed the Holy Spirit to do miracles on behalf of His message.

Ruby Slippers Training
Gospel of Mark 16: 15-20

I was reading in the gospels how Jesus not only cast demons out of people, but also healed the sick, and cured those with leprosy. He also imparted that same power and authority of the works He did upon those He sent out into local communities. Jesus said to His followers including all who would believe, that he wanted them to go out and preach this good news and these supernatural signs would follow. He said that if anyone believed, they would also cast out demons and heal the sick. The scriptures then say that the Holy Spirit worked with them in signs, wonders and miracles which confirmed their message. Because that happened for them, people turned their hearts to trust in Jesus and His message. More people followed Jesus and became disciples and future messengers as well.

Show Me the Power!

I was barely having any results with only a story to tell and some scriptures. I hardly knew the Bible at all so anyone who wanted to argue and reject my experience with Christ could easily do so. They knew a few scriptures as well and had their own twists on them but I had had this amazing experience. I didn't get saved by a Bible or in a church. I had an actual relational experience with God at the LGBT parade. No one could tell me that the Bible was wrong because I had this inner encounter with the Jesus the Bible talks about.

I began to cry out for God to back me up with these power demonstrations so that people would not only believe in Jesus but would also be able to "taste and see" that God was good.

I began to go deeper and press into God for more. I wanted so much to have this experience the disciples had. Jesus said communicated that His power wasn't just for special people but for anyone who truly follows Him.

Ruby Slippers Activate!

One day I heard that a supernatural training conference was coming to my hometown of Spokane. It was called "Healing Explosion." It was an equipping and training conference on how to activate your slippers–the Holy Spirit within you. They showed videos each night of a couple, Charles and Frances Hunter, who for many years experienced the power of the Spirit flowing through them healing the sick and doing the works of Christ.

There were times in the Old and New Testament where people would "fall" under the power of God's spirit. Sometimes these experiences were called trances. There are many instances throughout the Bible where people experienced this phenomena.

People have given these experiences their own names. I call them falling out under the power of the Spirit, trances or divine ecstasies. Some people experience love, joy, uncontrollable laughter and euphoria while in these holy states. This breaks off depression, anxiety, fear and so many negative emotions that seem to be so prevalent in these days. Countless people have been known to experience healings of the body, mind and emotions after falling out under the Spirit's power.

I've Got the Power!

I prayed for a friend of mine at this training conference who had been experiencing painful back problems. I commanded his back to align and he began to move about freely as the Holy Spirit corrected his back. It wasn't anything I was doing or he was doing. It was the power of God! I was amazed at such a small thing. The thought that God could heal someone through me was very exciting. I then prayed again for him and he fell to the floor under the power of the Spirit!

A little girl about ten years of age saw what had happened. She approached me and said she had lost all feeling in her leg from the kneecap down. I placed my hands upon her little leg and there she went! She fell to the floor under the power of God and all the feeling came back into her leg. Her mom was standing next to her when this happened. They were so shocked and gave all the praise to Jesus. I could hardly believe it. More people began approaching me for prayer and received some kind of powerful encounter or healing from God. I was in awe that God was flowing through me like this.

Gay Sex Worker Receives Wonderful Healing!

After the meeting I went downtown to the streets and began looking for people I could pray for. I started walking around what was called the "Fruit Loop" in Spokane. It was a hangout place for gay prostitutes. I saw a young man and introduced myself to him. I shared with him about how God had just used me for divine healings and asked if he needed healing for anything. I knew God would touch him. He consented. He told me he had painful arthritis in his foot. I bent down and placed my hand upon his foot and commanded the pain to leave in Jesus name. When I did that he fell out under the power of God on the sidewalk. When he got up he told me all of the pain was gone! He then prayed with me to receive Jesus into his heart. It was beautiful! This is what I was desiring in my prayers.

I needed my ruby slippers activated so people would know experientially that God and His Son Jesus loves, forgives and heals. Because he experienced God's touch, I didn't have to persuade him about the reality of God and Jesus. God healed him without any issues of him being gay or in male prostitution. God's love to the sinner is free and without obligation. Change can happen later after we begin to open our hearts to God's personal love. Change without God's love and power can produce just a religious person who tries to act like a Christian instead of having Christ within, flowing out. It is your choice to go deeper in the relationship. He is very much a gentleman and will never force Himself on you. He demonstrates His love first to draw us after Him. He makes Himself real at the start.

Migraine Vanishes!

That same night I went to a hospital to see a close friend of mine who was a maternity nurse. I told her everything that had happened that day. She was excited and introduced me to some nurses. One of them was having a migraine and asked me to pray for her. So I did. The power of God flowed from me to her and her migraine left suddenly.

I had this sense that in order to keep this flow going, I had to use it. I was beginning to learn how to use the power of this anointing from the ruby slippers. The wicked witch told Dorothy that she was the only one who knew how to use the power of the slippers. But she was wrong. Glinda began to train Dorothy on the road.

I was 23 years old and only four years old in Christ and was now beginning to learn how to operate and function in the ruby slippers I was wearing. I was also beginning to realize that I was truly a man of God, filled with the Holy Spirit. I went from gay to saint. Saints walk in the Spirit and do the works of Christ. Every person born of God is called a saint from day one.

The L.overs of G.od B.eing T.rue Members in the Church at Corinth (1 Corinthians)

I was beginning to see myself as a disciple of Christ with the power to heal the sick, and demonstrate the kingdom of God through signs and wonders that the Holy Spirit was accomplishing through me. This was such a radical new way of thinking about myself. I could hardly believe that God could take someone who had been called an abomination, unforgivable and useless to God, and turn them into a supernatural disciple of Christ. He will do the same for you. I read this amazing scripture in the Bible that explains how God uses people like me to later glorify the Lord.

Brothers, consider the time of your calling;
not many of you were wise by human standards; not
many were powerful; not many were of noble birth.
But God chose the foolish things of the world to shame
the wise. He chose the branded, stigmatized and the

*weak things of the world to shame the strong. He chose
the lowly and despised things of the world and the
things that are not, to nullify the things that are, so that
no one may boast in His presence.*

*It is because of Him that you are in Christ Jesus, who
has become for us wisdom from God; our righteousness,
holiness and redemption. Therefore, as it is written, let
him who boasts, boast in the Lord and not in their own
self-righteousness.*

1 Corinthians 1:26-31

Paul, who wrote this book, founded the church and lived there for one and half years. He knew these people and their backgrounds well as he affirmed them and how God was using them. [2]In Chapter 6, verses 8 and 9, he warns about a number of practices that preclude you from the Kingdom of God if you continue in them. That list included those who practice sexual immorality generally and adulterers as well as homosexual offenders and male prostitutes. In the next verse (verse 10) he says, "And <u>such were some of you</u>, but you were washed, but you were sanctified, but you were justified in the name of our Lord Jesus and by the Spirit of our God."

So the church at Corinth included LGBT (L.overs of G.od B.eing T.rue) members who came to Christ through God's power touching them through Paul's preaching in their community! Read this chapter and book. You will see they were in this congregation and they were all wearing the supernatural slippers! In fact, they were excelling in demonstrating the powers that they contained. They (with this rest of this Corinthian church) learned to experience and operate in all nine of the spiritual gifts. They learned faith, miracles, gifts of healings, prophetic words, words of knowledge, discerning of spiritual entities, tongues, interpretation of tongues

2 Lindsay, Scott. '1 Corinthians 1:1-9'. RPM, Volume 12, Number 12, March 21 to March 27 2010: http://old.thirdmill.org/newfiles/sco_lindsay/sco_lindsay.1Cor.002.pdf. Web. Accessed July 2017.

and words of wisdom. Paul's Grecian church members that included L.overs of G.od B.eing T.rue people were all very powerful in Christ! It was an early church Dorothy's Club! And all of the Christian world through history, including the modern-day Charismatic movement, has benefited from the letters of the apostle Paul instructing them how to fully operate in their supernatural ruby slippers!

A Closet-Gay Hippie Encounters Jesus

I had never heard of a young hippie preacher by the name of Lonnie Frisbee. He had been molested at a young age by a male babysitter which influenced him towards homosexuality. His parents didn't listen to him and he suffered alone. He was a dancer on the 70's teen show called Shabang and was also an artist attending the San Francisco Art Institute.

He was into LSD and metaphysical spirituality. Like many of the hippies, he abandoned the mainline American culture and wanted to find God. Lonnie, with some friends, headed for the Mojave Desert in California taking along some orange sunshine LSD. They also brought a Bible and read a story about John the Baptist who was baptizing the Jews in the Jordan River.

Lonnie decided, along with his friends, to get baptized in a nearby river while on acid. It was right after he had painted a beautiful picture of Jesus on a rock. He then stripped naked and walked into a cave right next to them. When he went into the cave he cried out with a loud voice, "God, if you're really real, reveal Yourself to me!" To Lonnie's great surprise and fear, power came into the cave like he had never experienced, on or off drugs. It scared him because he didn't really think anything would happen. Jesus appeared to him in a vision and showed him a picture of the southern California beach front with thousands and thousands of hippie youths being baptized and receiving Jesus as their Lord and Savior, similar to that of John the Baptist. It was interesting that he had just read about John the Baptist baptizing people in the river and then immediately after had a vision from Jesus calling him to baptize hippies in the ocean!

Jesus told Lonnie that He was calling him to be a messenger to these spiritually seeking hippies. Lonnie got his "ruby slippers" in that cave and began to go out by himself to Haight-Ashbury in San Francisco and the southern California beaches. He shared Jesus with Charles Manson, who rejected his invitation before Helter Skelter took place. He would stand on beach rocks and shout to all the hippies, "Come to God! Come to God!" He would pray for the hippies everywhere he went and supernatural healings and experiences would occur most of the time. He became what was later called a power evangelist. There is an amazing documentary about his life called *Lonnie Frisbee, The Life and Death of a Hippie Preacher*. He was the one who brought the historical hippie Jesus People movement to Calvary Chapel led by pastor Chuck Smith and then later to the renowned John Wimber, who, because of Lonnie's supernatural ministry, became known as the signs and wonders theologian. John Wimber's ministry was then called The Vineyard. Both ministries of Calvary Chapel and the Vineyard Christian Fellowship spread throughout the world because of Lonnie's gospel message and the power of the Holy Spirit through Lonnie's ruby slippers.

Lonnie, at times, felt unloved on a personal level from his spiritual fathers and felt used for his ruby slippers' anointing and effects for their church growth.

The glorious power that was coming through his ministry was affecting all of southern California and then spread throughout the world. This was all because he answered the call of God on his life with his whole heart. Lonnie later died from AIDS from sexual relapses. Why? No one really knows but it doesn't negate the fact that God was with him and used him mightily. God can use someone who struggles. It never means to use God's grace as an excuse to indulge in sexual immorality or promiscuity, but he never leaves us or forsakes us.

Lonnie struggled with his sexual identity, but he loved God with all of his heart and poured out every spiritual blessing he could through his faith and love for others. Even though he was the catalyst for the supernatural revivals of Christian movements, he was written out of their history books. Even though Lonnie struggled with, yet did not condone homosexuality, leaders were afraid to identify their growing denominations with him. If God can use Lonnie in a powerful way for love, He can use any of us who are reading this book.

Remember that in this former letter from the First Corinthians church, God chose the branded and the despised on purpose. It was so no one could say God used them because they were good and moral, noble, educated or rich people. God chooses whomever He wants and He forgives anyone and everyone if they desire it through faith in Jesus.

Unbelievers Class at Calvary Chapel

I was invited to a Calvary Chapel New Believers class held on a Wednesday night in my hometown. I had been in a relationship with Jesus for only a few years, but I was not just a new believer of the word but a doer of the word. There were many classes going on in the downstairs hallway of this large church building. I had never been there before.

The leader of this class began to teach the "newbies" in Christ that supernatural signs, wonders and miracles weren't for today but only happened during the historical time of Jesus and the apostles. He didn't know anything about the signs and wonders ministry of Lonnie Frisbee that was the catalyst for this world-wide church denomination!

This teacher was completely ignorant of the power of God that was responsible for the existence of the very church he was teaching in. (I can't say he represents all of the teachers/leaders in this denomination.) There's a word for this kind of unbelief. It's called "cessationism." They say that the gifts of the Spirit ceased after the days of the original apostles. It's a very misguided, false teaching that isn't from God, nor is it in the Bible. It keeps God's people as dwarfed Munchkins.

As he was teaching this new believers class on how not to believe in the power of God today, I just had to raise my hand. He invited me to talk and I shared with him and the class about the supernatural experiences I was having around town. I told them that the Holy Spirit was healing people through me on the streets, in the hospital and throughout different locations. He was taken back to say the least. To my surprise, he then asked me if I'd like to pray for people to have encounters from God after his class.

When his class was over he dismissed everyone. I didn't under-stand, as I had thought I was going to pray for people in the class and see what God might do for them. Instead he went down the hall and invited around 11 other Bible study teachers. I wondered if he was really sincere or if he just wanted to prove his point. I was a bit nervous yet excited to see what God would do. I asked God to back me up because I would be very embarrassed if He didn't.

There I was standing in faith to believe in front of these teach-ers. I asked these leaders if any of them had ever received the Holy Spirit's gift of tongues according to historical passages in the book of Acts and First Corinthians. None of them raised their hand, which meant no. I then asked them to raise their hands if they would be open for this gift, which to my surprise they did. I then shared a few scriptures about what it was and how to receive it, either by the laying on of hands or just by God Himself. In this meeting I was going to lay my hand on their head as the apostles did in the Bible. The first person came to the front of the room. I didn't lay my hand on him but just lightly touched his forehead with my index finger. Down he went! He fell out under the power of the Holy Spirit speaking in heavenly tongues on the floor! You could feel the shock and awe in the room. Then another leader came up and the same thing happened. One after another they all came forward and ended up on the floor in divine trances speaking in Holy Spirit tongues. The Spirit even started touching people sitting down without me even praying for them. One woman began to say, "What's happening to me, I'm shaking!" She was shaking from the power of God on her. I told her that God's power was touching her and for her to come to the front of the room for more. She worked her way to the front and I put my finger on her head. She started to go down while shaking in the power and grabbed onto some chairs to keep herself from falling. It didn't work. The power of God pressed her to the floor while she was flopping like a fish, speaking in tongues. I even prayed for the teacher's wife. She went down as well speaking in tongues. The teacher's jaw just about hit the floor. I then turned to him, eye to eye, and asked if he would like to also get the baptism of the Spirit. He said, "yes" and I prayed with him. Nothing happened. Because he probably taught it so often, it was difficult for him to come to the realization that God's signs, wonders and miracles are alive and well today. He saw every single Bible teacher he had invited into this room be prayed for (by someone similar to Lonnie Frisbee) laying on the floor speaking in tongues under the power of God! It was an amazing, impacting and incredibly fun night!

Chapter 11

The Yellow Brick Road

*God Has Good Works Planned in Advance For Us
Even Before We Arrive.*

Ephesians 1:4

The Good Witch shows Dorothy the Yellow Brick Road that is now "over the rainbow" and informs her that it should take her back home. She begins to take small steps on the spiraling road that doesn't seem to make sense. It's not straight. What she doesn't realize is that this pathway for her life was predestined before she was ever born. Her realization as a new creation saint along with divine purpose would occur throughout this journey.

Before my encounter with God I used to think that the only way I could be a Christian was if I were straight instead of gay. After my divine encounter with God, I discovered that the way wasn't as straight as I thought it would be. What was interesting is that God spoke to my heart at the gay parade. He told me that He wasn't asking me to change but to surrender. He told me put my trust in Him and to follow Him. This meant to surrender to His path...to His Yellow Brick Road. It was to be a walk He had for me that would begin my spiritual transformation.

He wasn't asking me to go straight. He was asking me to go saint! Straight up! I was oriented towards being gay. I thought gay thoughts and had gay habits and feelings. I had to put my trust in Jesus and follow Him. That's all He asked me to do at the time. He basically said, "Do your best and I'll do the rest. Learn to get to know Me."

I was told that if you press into God through different kinds of prayer and singing to Him, you could have deeper encounters and relationship with God. This happens through the inward relationship with the Holy Spirit. I began to have spiritual encounters.

Divine Ecstasy!

Ec-sta-sy
Rapture, bliss, elation, euphoria
an emotional or trance-like state, originally involving an
experience of mystic self-transcendence.
(definition from Wikipedia)

One day I was determined to spend an entire day praying and earnestly seeking an encounter with God. I prayed in tongues out loud in my living room for hours. It was daunting and I did stop here and there to breathe. But something actually happened! It was like warm euphoric peace flowed down from the top of my head throughout my entire being. I could feel it in my natural body senses as well. I could hardly believe it! I didn't understand what the experience meant at the time but it clearly told me that I was encountering the love of God in an incredible way through the Holy Spirit. It felt like a powerful tranquil spiritual ecstasy similar to a chemically induced experience I had with crystal meth in San Francisco!

There's a scripture in Romans which says that God pours out His love into our hearts through the power of the Holy Spirit! Praying in tongues can help us to encounter God's love like this.

Throughout my journey God was going to show me my place in Him with spiritual encounters through His abundant grace. Two meanings of grace are: undeserved favor and divine enablement. It was amazing to experience and difficult to believe God loved me in this way. My mind had a hard time assimilating His forgiveness. Each time I felt His infusions of grace, I had to remind myself that He loved me and wasn't angry at me for my sins. That belief was difficult to sink in. It still is sometimes but I understand that this is why Jesus came.

Paul's letter to the Roman Christian church stated that where sin abounded, God's grace would abound even more. Where my life was full of sins from the past, or even later when struggling or falling into something not good and right, God's favor and love would match it all through His mercy and grace. He treated me like a cherished son. This is what Jesus was like with sinners, lepers, outcasts and alcoholics. He ate and drank with them as a close friend. God Himself hung out with the despised, the brokenhearted, the lonely, the stigmatized, the branded and the rejects of society. The religious clergy went crazy over it and denounced Him as a demon, a glutton and a sinner. I doubt they would venture into a gay bar or a drag show to hang out and socialize with LGBT.

Mercy is like a police officer ripping up your traffic ticket. The death of Christ showed mercy as it pardoned us from our sins. Grace is like the same police officer writing you a check for $100,000 on top of it! Being given the Ruby Slippers of eternal riches is the grace given to us along with the forgiveness of our sins.

I still felt, thought and acted gay, accompanied by sexual behaviors at times. Sexual experiences had become not only a habit for me but a lifestyle, so it wasn't easy to just suddenly act or feel like a saint, as the Bible calls us. Being a "saint" is a process of transformation from the inside out, but I knew I needed to change some of my outward behaviors. We have to change many of our outward environments, friends and things we do to make it easier to become the new creation that God has made us. Our minds can't comprehend the new reality of who we are if we're living in the old reality of who we were.

Dancing Queen Has a Spiritual Ecstasy in Cornwall, England

Throughout the years I have learned the secret of what I call "divine guidance and divine appointments." This is what the book of Ephesians in the Bible means by "being created for good works planned in advance." (Ephesians 2:10) God has an unfolding purpose for L.overs of G.od B.eing T.rue!

In the mid 90's I was co-hosting a team with Glorian Bonnette in Cornwall, England. We've led a few teams there throughout the years. Cornwall is below Wales. Our mission base was in a beautiful gardened mansion called the Treyloyan Manor. It was located in St. Ives. St. Ives is a beautiful idyllic artist and fisherman community on the sea.

One night a few of our team members wanted to walk the streets with me to see how God guides me in divine guidance along with divine appointments. Glorian had her own word for this. She calls them "Godcidences," instead of coincidences.

As we were waking down the cobblestone narrow streets, I noticed a dance club called the Isobar. I felt an inner impulse to go in there.

I told my team that I felt an inner intuitive impression to go in there. A few of my team had a hard time going into a bar because of Christian traditional mindsets that you don't go into places like that. Jesus ate and drank with sinners, so to me, that means he did frequent places where people who drank were. He hung out with them, became their friend and worked miracles among them. I like to do what Jesus did. It's called, WWJD. (What would Jesus do?)

A few people from my team broke off to walk the streets instead. The ones who stayed with me wanted to break out of religious traditional evangelism methods and knew that I was a horse of a different color, so they wanted to ride that horse. They were letting me train them on how Jesus would do it. Jesus followed his inner guidance and ended up hanging out with people of disrepute even to the questioning of his own disciples and religious leaders.

Jesus' first miracle was turning water into wine at a wedding. This is interesting because as I will share, a wedding party was happening in this nightclub.

When we went in, the nightclub was empty with only a few people. My friends and I got a table and ordered something. They thought I must have missed it and I know they began to instantly think that I didn't hear God and maybe we should have gone with the others. One of them was carrying a big cross to draw attention, similar to the way a man used to do it in the 70's named Arthur Blessitt. I'm not one to copy models on reaching people for Christ anymore. They helped before I learned to kick in to trusting the Spirit in my heart and not my mind. It has become a lot more exciting this way, and more effective for me in reaching hearts for God. Whatever it takes to draw attention to the message! Not to judge others for their ways, but I have to say that I'm truly thankful for the wisdom that I've developed through experience, mixed with heartfelt love for people.

I got up on the dance floor by myself, since no one else was there and began to pray while dancing. I was having a private dialogue with God. I told him, I think something should happen here. I really felt You guiding me in here and this group is wanting to experience divine guidance. I'm going to leave this place now because of the lack of patience with my team, so if You have brought me here, I need You to do something between here and the exit door. I then stopped dancing and praying and told my team that we could go. Feeling a bit awkward, we began to leave the joint. My credibility for being a cutting edge Spirit-led evangelist was also going out the door!

But as we were a few feet from the exit door, out of nowhere steps this young lady. She stands directly in front of me looking straight into my eyes. She asked me where I was going. It was great! I knew exactly what was happening. This was our first divine appointment. I told her that we were leaving and then I framed a question to her. I said, "We're leaving. Why do you ask? Do you want us to stay?" She answered quite emphatically, "Yes. I do." I told her that we would be doing that. And then she walked away. God saved me. My team just saw a sign that caused them to wonder. I turned around to see her walk up a flight of stairs that we hadn't seen when we walked in. I decided to follow her and so we did. When we got upstairs, there was another dance floor, but this one was completely crowded with loud music, laser lights and a complete light show!

We found a place to sit in the crowd and I asked God what to do next. The spirit in me said to go find that lady and ask her to dance. So I did. I found her alone in the crowd and I asked her to dance. She was happy to do that.

As we're dancing, introductions happened. She asked me where I was from. I told her the United States. She then asked what brought me to St. Ives. I shared with her that I was a Christian missionary and was there with a team. She lit up! She laughed and then told me that she used to go to a charismatic church in Penzance. I then lit up! I told her that I ministered in her church with our team just a couple of years ago in Penzance. This is where the famous movie, *The Pirates of Penzance*, was set. She asked me if I had ever seen anyone fall out under the power of God when prayed for. I was getting excited now because this was obviously a divine appointment. I told her that it happens often when I pray for people. I then asked her if she'd ever seen gold dust show up on her hands. She said no, but would love to experience that. Immediately after she said that, I checked out my hands to see if a few golden sparkles might begin to appear as they often do, because of practicing the presence of God like I do much of the time. Gold sparkles appear on and in my skin at times and it transfers to people around me. It's a sign that makes people wonder. I then get to share about Jesus and His love, with less arguments because whoever I'm with (many times) sees something supernatural and they listen rather than argue. God wants to make it easy for people. That's why the scriptures say to "taste and see that the Lord is good." (Psalm 34:8) Experience first, faith second for the unbeliever. Signs, wonders and miracles are to follow those who believe so that people can believe in the good news that Jesus Christ came into the world and took our sins upon Himself He did this so that we could be forgiven, cleansed and dignified as those re-created in His divine image. We go from merely being fallen humanity to heavenly sons and daughters of God. Paul the apostle said that he shared the gospel of Jesus Christ with demonstrations of the Spirit's power so that men's faith wouldn't be upon man's philosophies and wisdom, but upon God's power.

So, as I looked at my fingertips, which is where they usually start to sparkle on my hands, I saw a few of them begin to appear. It wasn't much but enough to see. I showed her and she excitedly asked me if God might give her some as well. I said, "Of course He will!" Let's look. As she opened her hands and began to look on her fingertips, little golden sparkles began to appear in front of her eyes. She watched them appear.. One here, another there, and more started to sparkle. She screamed in delight and awe. Since her heart was so open to God's fun love with her, I spoke a word that I felt God had for her. I just told her how much God loved her and that He was with her in her hard times, just as much if not even more in the times when she was doing well. I also told her that God has not abandoned her and sent me in here to dance with her, because Jesus was wanting to dance with her.

Immediately after I spoke that inspired word to her, which the Bible calls prophesy, which encourages, strengthens and builds up someone's faith, the power of God came all over her. She fell out under the power of God in the middle of the crowded dance floor, shaking and vibrating on the floor. She was laughing and rolling around. She was having a divine ecstasy from her Lord and Savior! This was so dramatic, that the bouncers had to come over and pull her off the floor. They must have thought that she had a drug or alcohol overdose!

After she was dragged off the floor, she barely got up and began to stagger around the room to show and tell her friends what was happening. She would show them the golden sparkles on her hands while she was staggering as though drunk. I have to say now, that she was drunk, but not on Vodka. She was drunk on Godka! Similar to the believers in the second chapter of Acts, they were staggering around and speaking in tongues when they got filled with the Holy Spirit. Thousands of onlookers from the Jewish festival in the streets saw and heard this commotion. They mocked them and said out loud that they must be drunk. Peter spoke up and told them that it was too early in the morning, being only nine o'clock. He then explained that they were having a spiritual experience that was prophesied from Joel and Jesus about the coming of the Holy Spirit that would cause people to have visions, dreams, prophecy and salvation!

This lady staggered around as though drunk, and laughing, going from friend to friend. My friend Freddie who was with me, came to me to watch this amazing sight. I told her to watch me. I would blow toward the lady who was a distance away and she would suddenly fall out under the power of God in front of her friends. This happened around eight times. And she was never facing me when this happened. She had no clue that God and I were having a lot of fun with her so that her friends would see this sign that was making them wonder. She would later share with them about her experience with me, and how she got a word that told her that Jesus loved and adored her.

That night, a bridesmaids' party came in all dressed up from a wedding. As they began to dance in a circle, the song, "Dancing Queen," sung by Abba, began to play. The Lord began to share with me that His dancing queen is in the night clubs. He told me that I represented her spiritual Lover, Jesus, who is called the Bridegroom of the church. He began to share with me that Jesus, through me, danced with His Bride, His dancing queen. A scripture came to my mind in Psalm 139:8 that says, "Where can I flee from Your presence? If I make my bed in hell, You are there."

I then saw another lady dressed up in solid black with bright red lips. She was standing next to the dancing queen that Jesus and I danced with. She was glaring at me with evil eyes. I could tell that she was very angry about something. She knew spiritually that something was going on and was obviously a spiritually discerning person, but she was coming from another source. I think the Wicked Witch of the West was working with her. In fact, I'm quite sure of it. She grabbed her friend and began to french kiss her so that I could see that they were lovers. I got it. They were lesbians. She felt threatened. Jesus was the dancing queen's lover and this lady became gravely jealous. She knew who Jesus was and knew that she was probably going to lose her lover to God. If this lady in black loved God, she would have been very happy. But she wasn't. She wouldn't let me get near God's dancing queen for the rest of the night. I didn't stay long after that. The mission was accomplished. The good work planned in advance happened. We all got to see how Jesus loves lesbians, but not all lesbians love Jesus. It's the same for us all. We are all God's dancing queens, but will we all dance with Him? Let's do it! Let's dance! Put on your Ruby dance shoes and dance the blues! (Bowie)

Gold Sparkle Activation!

If you are in direct sunlight or near a lamp, open the palms of your hands facing the direct light. Look steadily on the skin on your fingertips. Watch for little golden or silver sparkles begin to appear in your skin. Look closely and patiently. The presence of God may cause this to appear on your skin as though he were giving you a little hug. Don't think He doesn't love you if it doesn't happen. Just check it out here and there as you're reading this book. You don't even have to believe. Just open your heart to God and let him enjoy you and show himself to you in little ways like this. Send me an email and share your experiences with me. If it happens, go and show your friends under sunlight and God may give it to them as well. Who knows? Sometimes I get sparkles that include the colors of the rainbow! They appear at times all over the palms of my hands and sometimes on my forehead as I'm sharing the gospel with people!

Chapter 12

The Scarecrow

The Scarecrow and the Mind of Christ

When Dorothy met the scarecrow, he informed her that he didn't have a brain. Dorothy told him to join her, because the Wizard might have one for him. He agreed and joined her on the Yellow Brick Road.

Probably because of drug use in my past, my brain wasn't functioning as fully and normally as it could have. I would have avoided many of the things I did in life and thought more about their consequences. But because of brokenness and a wounded heart, my brain didn't care too much about the results of my many foolish actions. I had no hope as a result of my formative home years in Kansas to think that it mattered much. I already believed I was doomed to failure. I had no inclination toward any real success when I left home as a lost boy without faith.

I used to be good at things in elementary school, but as my self esteem began to decline, so did my desire to learn. I began to drink alcohol and smoke marijuana in junior high as a result of peer pressure. This also caused me to not excel in school.

When I was translated to Oz, the Kingdom of Light, I began to discover that another mind was given to me that could not decay. It was the very mind of Christ! The mind of Christ always uses 100% of it's capacity and I would learn to tap into this new mind that came into me.

Let this mind be in you, which was also in Christ Jesus.
Philippians 2:5

For who hath known the mind of the Lord, that he may
instruct Him? But we have the mind of Christ.
1 Corinthians 2:16

At the age of 19, I had returned to my hometown of Spokane after my encounter with God. I began to discover soon after that experience that I must have been over the rainbow. I felt a new kind of love and peace inside myself and saw a colorful world, such like I had never seen. In a previous chapter I had written about my friend who I went in search of to help me in my new journey. I needed his help to guide me. He believed that what I told him was true. He began to share with me about another experience I could have which he called the baptism of the Holy Spirit. He showed me in the Bible how believers could receive a spiritual prayer language that could help me experience the presence of God and to understand His thoughts. He called it the gift of tongues.

After my friend Chris prayed for me to receive the gift of the Holy Spirit, I received my prayer language. In 1 Corinthians, chapter 14, it says that when we pray to ourselves in the Spirit, such as tongues, that our spirit is built up, edified and developed. The apostle Paul challenged his Corinthian, L.ove G.od B.e T.rue church to pray in tongues often. When they did it helped them to activate all of the other spiritual gifts and to experience intimacy with God.

Praying in Tongues and the Mind of Christ

The more I prayed in the Spirit, the more I could discern the thoughts of God from my own. They carried a tranquil peace when these thoughts flowed into my mind. I discovered in the Bible that not only can you speak in tongues but you can also sing in tongues to receive understanding of the thoughts of Christ.

In the early 90's, while in Corvallis, Oregon, I was praying in my prayer language. As I was doing this I felt impressed to hold my own Christian revival meetings which would consist of leading worship, preaching the word and praying for people for Holy Spirit encounters. I also discerned that this was to be done six nights a week for three months. I then heard God reveal to me that He would have a special reward upon completion of this task. These impressions, directions and strategies came from the thoughts of God to me, which is the mind of Christ.

I stepped out in faith and asked my pastor if he would give me access to his building to do these meetings six nights a week for three months. He agreed because he saw that God had a special calling on my life and wanted to be a part of it. He gave me the keys to his church and I began the meetings!

During these three months of leading praise and worship with my guitar, teaching, prophesying, and praying for people, something new and wonderful would happen every single night! People had God encounters on the floor. They had visions and would hear His voice. Divine healings and baptisms of the Holy Spirit would happen as well. One night a youth group across the hall came in and they all received the gift of tongues while falling out under the power of God on the floor! It was funny because the youth group leader wasn't into the power of God and wanted to use psychology to develop his youth group. Oops! He was not too happy that they had encounters with God outside of his psychology class. I'm a believer in many aspects of psychology and thank God for it, but psychology can't baptize people in the Holy Spirit.

After this three month assignment was complete a woman felt led to send me to Russia with a well known international Bible teacher and supernatural Evangelist named Marilyn Hickey. She asked if I would go and she would also pay my way. It was hard to believe. I had never in my life imagined I would go to Russia. Already God was doing exceedingly more than I could have imagined. This was the "reward" that the mind of Christ revealed to me when I had prayed in regards to the three months of service.

Off I flew on my first international flight to Moscow. A team of about 200 Christians from around America joined Marilyn's team. We stayed in a five star hotel and ministered to Russians in unused former KGB buildings. Marilyn learned that I loved to dance spontaneously during music. She asked me to dance in the streets as her musicians played and while other team members handed out Christian leaflets written in Russian. They were so hungry for this information about Jesus that we would be practically mobbed to get a leaflet. Busses pulled up and I would quickly board them and give them to all the passengers. After one of the services many that attended lined up in the lobby for me to pray for them. They all fell out on the floor of the lobby under the power of God!

After returning from Russia I was invited to join her team again, this time in Israel. I was blown away! All this came from praying in the Spirit, and hearing God's voice to have those small meetings every day for three months!

The Tomb of Jesus

One of the first stops on our ministry tour in Israel was an excavated Roman outdoor amphitheater in Caesarea Philippi. Our tour guide asked our large touring group if anyone would like to go onto the stage and sing a song because of the great acoustics. My heart was beating fast because I love to release songs of the Lord but decided to let a group of ladies who had raised their hands sing a song. Because we were a group bringing the gospel of Jesus Christ and representing Marilyn Hickey Ministries, I assumed they would sing a song about God. But no! They started singing of all songs, "Old McDonald had a farm."...and on his farm he had some pigs...E-I-E-I-O!" Here we were in front of tourists from all over the world and having such an opportunity to glorify God. It was very inappropriate, especially because Jews don't eat pork!

Feeling a bit of hot steam seething in my heart because of that inappropriate song, I quickly raised my hand. The tour guide invited me to go up and sing something. Yes! Now was my time to really share something meaningful. We were in Israel, the Holy Land! I got up on stage, took a deep breathe, raised my hands to God and like a trumpet released a song called, "He's the Mighty One of Israel". The lyrics are about Christ bringing healing, refreshing and His favor to His people. You could tangibly feel the presence of God begin to permeate the air and people could sense it. It created an impact. In fact, Marilyn Hickey noticed it and asked me to lead worship with my guitar in other places on this ministry tour. I was elated!

Later, I found myself leading worship at the very tomb of Jesus for a communion service. It was also my birthday.

I was then invited to lead worship at the Jordan River where Jesus got baptized by John the Baptist. Everyone, including myself, got baptized there. From there I led worship at the wall of Jericho, Jerusalem Bible College and other locations. When I returned home to the states, I received phone calls from surprised friends of mine who saw me on Marilyn's TV program singing at the Jordan River.

While singing with my guitar in the lobby of a five star hotel in Jerusalem, an older Jewish Rabbi came to me and said that he felt as though I was a "psalmist in Israel." He asked for my number and told me he was the head of a nursing home in New York for older holocaust victims. I gave him my number. He later sent me a letter informing me that he was gay and wanted me to be his lover and asked if I'd travel with him to the Greek Isles. Wow! I was not expecting that and declined the offer. But it did touch my heart that my music and God's presence touched this gay Rabbi's heart. I know that because the true song and light that he was attracted to in me was the light and music of Jesus.

To Russia Again, With Love!

I was invited again to go to Russia with Marilyn Hickey's ministry team. This time my friend Grace and her son went with me. It was amazing! We spent time on a Russian cruise down the Volga River with underground Russian pastors. I brought along my coffee maker and my special coffee beans to bless these amazing men. I also led worship with my guitar on this cruise ship.

A Vision of Aladdin's Magic Carpet

When I was in Jerusalem with Marilyn's team, I took a cab to a church where a woman by the name of Ruth Ward Heflin ministers as a prophet. She wrote a book called *Glory* that influenced my life and ministry.

I called her church and asked if I could do a dance worship presentation at their service. Ruth was very much into these creative expressions although she would not be there that evening. So off I went with my dance costume in tow. After the presentation they were very encouraging with prophetic words for me.

When I returned home to Oregon after my mission trip in Israel, I went to a conference where Ruth Heflin was the keynote speaker. Once again, I wore my dance outfit because there is always spontaneous dancing in these kinds of conferences. I was in the back of the room and was tapped on the shoulder by some elders and asked not to dance. I think they must have thought I was gay. Lol...

I got that kind of treatment quite frequently in Christian worship gatherings. I call it the LGBT shoulder tap. It would always hurt a little, sometimes not so little, because I felt their condemnation. They didn't know me and yes, I can still came across as gay, even though God calls me a saint. I didn't go horizontal. I went vertical....straight up! I have peace with God through Jesus Christ. That's good enough for me.

As Ruth Heflin was playing the piano and singing on stage she had a prophetic vision which she began to share with the audience. She said, "there is a young man backstage waving a blue banner, singing and dancing. I saw you in a vision waving your blue streamer-banner. It then turned into a magic carpet like in the movie Aladdin. You were sitting on it and it flew you to the continent of South Africa." She then said, "As you sing and dance as God inspires you, those songs, movements and dances will carry you to the nations!" Wow! That was hard to believe.

I had been shoulder tapped and humiliated and then God publicly honored me and gave me a word about going to the nations from this amazing woman of God! I love it when others judge you and then God honors you! This is what is so fun for me now. I can be put down by religious people but God gives me blessings afterward to show them that no one is better than anyone else. God was also telling me He was pleased with me and my dancing for Christ. They wanted to look good before men and I wanted to look good before God. It's like the verse in Psalm 23 where it says "He (the Good Shepherd) prepares a table before me in the presence of my enemies."

Flying on God's Carpet to South Africa

About a year after Ruth's prophetic word I found myself as a keynote speaker at the large international dome in Nairobi, Kenya. I've spoken there a few times over the years. Nairobi is located in the eastern part of Africa. Ruth Heflin's word to me was about South Africa.

One night during the conference a song began to quietly play in my spirit. I got up and went to the microphone and sang it aca-pella. I called it "He's the Mighty One of Kenya." After I sang this song one of the speakers came to the microphone and shared that I sounded exactly like the South Africans! He then shared that he felt I should fly that week to South Africa to minister in any way I felt led. I jumped on Jesus' magic carpet and flew to the continent of South Africa exactly as Ruth Heflin had seen in her vision.

All of this that I have written in this chapter and more, came through praying in the Spirit thus, receiving understanding.

Because of my obedience and stepping out in faith, I was rewarded as God said I would be. It was beyond my wildest imagination that I would be so privileged to travel and minister in Russia, Israel, South and East Africa, along with finances that came my way to accomplish it all.

> *We continually ask God to fill you with the knowledge*
> *of his will through all the wisdom and understanding*
> *that the Spirit gives.*
>
> *Colossians 1 :9*

Chapter 13

The Tin Woodman

The Tin Woodman and the Heart of God

Dorothy is meeting new friends along the Yellow Brick Road. She is discovering that each of these friends represent something new from God. One of these friends is the Tin Woodman. In the Old Testament, Ezekiel 35:26 says that the spirit of God would turn hearts of stone into tender hearts of flesh. That's what we get when the love of God pours into us through the power of the indwelling Holy Spirit.

Since the night I received Jesus at the gay parade, I began to experience His tangible love and presence infusing my heart. I would read books from people like Thomas Merton, Madame Jeanne Guyon, Brother Lawrence and Theresa of Ávila as they taught the inward ways of prayer in the heart. Books from these Catholic saints and mystics helped me to learn this. I also learned how to forgive those who hurt me and how to do good to them and to bless them in return. That wasn't easy, but as I did it over and over again, I began to gain back my heart, my peace and my joy. Bitterness held me captive. It caused me to not care about myself and to view myself as a victim. Without knowing it, I now realize that deep-rooted bitterness is actually against God, even though we may not recognize it. It says, "How could God allow me to be hurt so much by people and society. I'm a good person." I think it may be fueled by a belief that says a good God can't allow bad things to happen, especially to me. Then self pity comes into play which is a horrible challenge to overcome. Over the years as I practiced receiving love from God and others, as well as direct experience with God's love and peace flowing into my being, my heart softened and was transformed by His love. This is what the Bible means by the word "Christ-like." God is love. Love becomes like a river that flows out to the world.

Broken Rainbow

In 2009, I had just come out of a 30 day inpatient treatment center from a drug relapse. I had been clean for over 20 years. I relapsed into a two year progressive meltdown into old sexual and drug behaviors.

God's love and presence was infused in me fresh and new every morning while I was in the inpatient program. I was very broken again, but in this brokenness I didn't feel alone. I had many years of relationship with God and we were close. I knew He loved me. When I was released, I continued to go to various outpatient therapy groups to work on issues of my heart that had never been fully healed. I didn't want to struggle with sexual and/or drug addictions that came through reactions to life's pains anymore.

I knew God's love was completely unconditional. And because I was His child, whenever I would fall, I could get back up again in God's love and mercy and receive His forgiveness. I discovered that Jesus' blood flows unceasingly like a river through our hearts and consciousness. So many times I felt I had gone too far and crossed the lines of forgiveness and I would feel extremely afraid. The fact that I even cared about crossing God's lines meant God's spirit had not left me. You can't feel broken and anxious about losing God if you don't love God. Just because we sin and fall short on the Yellow Brick Road doesn't mean we don't love God with all our hearts. He knows our frailties and our weaknesses. His grace helps us to get up so that we can continue on the Yellow Brick

Road in righteous freedom. God's heart can be grieved because we're in a relationship. I have grieved God's heart before, and it's painful.

The Holy Spirit, Glinda, is always our helper in times of need. God's continual love has never ceased to blow my mind. Whenever I have been faithless, He has always remained faithful. God comes to me with tangible gentleness and kindness when I come to Him with a broken and sincere heart with regard to my failures. He wipes away every tear. He also stores our precious tears in bottles. He must have many vats full of my tears. This journey has not been easy. Jesus said that the road was narrow and few travel it. There is pain you go through that is difficult but the transformation and rewards far outweigh them all. It takes great courage and humility. Real L.overs of G.od B.eing T.rue walk the road least travelled.

A Dream about Addicts Loving God

I had a dream from God about Madame Jeanne Guyon, the Catholic woman whose books I've read on how to pray inwardly to experience union with God. In the dream I was walking through the halls of an inpatient drug and alcohol treatment center. In every client's hands was her book, *Experiencing the Depths of Jesus Christ*. I was taken aback by that. I then saw a few people who had another one of her more advanced books called, *Union with God*. I began to weep in the dream because all these broken people were reading her books on learning how to know and love God. In the dream these people in rehab were broken, even as I had been, and some much more. They ran from God because of guilt, shame and fear. They were afraid of God, yet here they were, each one having these spiritual books on prayer.

I asked the guide in the dream who had given these people these books and he motioned for me to follow him. He took me up a staircase to a small room, where I saw a French woman with black hair wearing a dark blue dress. It was Madame Jeanne

Guyon! I was in awe. She looked into my eyes as a son, placed her hand upon my head and imparted a commission to help addicts of all kinds experience the spiritual depths of Jesus Christ. She was a devout Catholic Christian and was thrown in the Bastille Prison in France for helping so many people know God for themselves outside of religion. You can order her books on Seedsowers.com.

Rainbow Rising

All the pain I experienced in life healed and mixed with tranquil peace in Christ. It produced a love messenger that was about to walk the streets of Spokane again. This would be much different than my former bullhorn evangelism which was inspired more from youthful zeal. I began to walk the streets in this new emerging love which began to take over my heart and soul. As I walked the downtown Spokane streets I listened to God and began to let His heart for the broken people of the inner city flow into my heart. I took city buses instead of driving. I wanted to connect and identify with these precious people bringing God's heart. Glinda, the Holy Spirit, would begin to reveal things to me about individuals as I walked the streets. I was able to perceive which ones would later receive Jesus and the baptism of the Holy Spirit.

There was one man that I saw standing on the sidewalk of his downtown apartment. God had spoken to me a year before I prayed with him that I would meet him and later be his pastor. This happened and he opened his apartment for "home church." We grew in numbers and moved locations. We met at Riverfront Park in the summer then in a downtown boxing studio. I met an inner city pastor who had a church in this art gallery storefront. I was walking by praying about our next church and outreach location. We went out for breakfast and I shared with him about my life and ministry downtown. He invited me to host whatever I wanted in his beautiful gallery. It had a stage, kitchen, bathrooms, sound system and two video screens. This pastor didn't know me. He felt a trust about me and called my pastor for a reference who gave him a wonderful recommendation. That meant a great deal to me. It healed another part of my heart to be promoted by a spiritual father.

I began at that location on a Saturday morning with "Higher Power Church." I based the name on AA's concept of Higher Power so that addicts would feel welcome to come and not feel any pressure to be "Christian." I played acoustic guitar and sang and was accompanied by a flautist, drummer and an electric guitarist. We let the Spirit flow through the music so that people coming in could experience the sweet presence of God. We didn't have a traditional Sunday church model. We just let love flow spontaneously through the gifts of the Spirit.

My First Light Club– "The Reign-bow Electric House of Prayer"

Also on Sunday nights I started my first inner city Light Club forming a band; I would just sing to God while the others played spontaneously. I would also play lead guitar at times. I called these Sunday night meetings, "The REHOP," meaning The Reign-bow Electric House of Prayer. We yielded to the spontaneous words of God flowing through us to sing to people instead of preaching at them. Preaching the inspired words of God to people, instead of at them did happen at times, but our times together were mostly singing to spontaneous music played by a rockish-jazz type band.

Burning Spokane

One day God gave me a strategy to reach the entire downtown street and homeless community. The name, "Burning Spokane" came to my mind. I met a new friend named Jeff, who had an idea about putting up posters and handing out flyers. I posted them on poles downtown and handed out flyers to the downtown street and homeless people. I turned the REHOP music prayer night into a bimonthly barbecue block party and clothing giveaway.

We also gave out raffle tickets and had laser light shows! I invited people to come up front to share the powerful experiences they were having with Jesus and His power working in their lives. Lines wrapped around the block with all types of people–different races, religions and sexual orientations (LGBT)–coming regularly. Some Christians reading this would ask me the question as they typically do, "Did they repent of their sins or did they change their lifestyles?" My answer to that is, some did on their own later by going into inpatient treatment centers, the dream center or Victory outreach which were live-in discipleship houses. But the REHOP and Burning Spokane outreaches were intended to love on people unconditionally, feed and clothe them as well as giving them opportunities to experience the supernatural presence of God, divine encounters, healings and miracles. The Bible says to "Taste and see that God is good." (Psalm 34:8)

Without sampling a food, why would anyone want to buy that food and change their diet? Jesus touched many people with His love and power just because He loved them without requiring change. We have found that change comes because people want to and choose to change, not by any of us putting guilt on anyone to change their lifestyles. To this day, two years later after the REHOP closed down due to the building being bought out by another business, people come to me from the streets of downtown telling me of their lives becoming better, along their strengthened faith and walk with Christ! The effects of God's unconditional love and power in many lives after the street ministry still amaze me! They were impacted by the strange unconditional love that many of them were not accustomed to. In order to get food in several ministries they first had to listen to Bible preaching over and over again, and we discerned many hearts seemed dull to the gospel. We felt led to do it differently. Our approach was hugging, food, music and demonstrations of God's power. Many of the people would just sit on the sidewalk outside enjoying the food and the social aspect. No one had to sit inside, listen or participate. It was a safe place and the coolest hangout downtown.

Halo!

At the REHOP, a young, gay African-American guy named Jay came and asked if he could sing "Halo" from Beyonce. I agreed. After he sang I asked him if it would be OK to lay hands on him so that he would possibly experience a touch from God. He agreed not knowing what to expect. The power and love of God came over him and he went down to the floor in divine ecstasy! He got up staggering like a drunk! He had to get a ride home from someone because he got so drunk in the spirit of God that he could hardly stand up! He kept coming back weekly and had encounters every time. He said it was the first time he had ever felt God's love and power like that in his life. I think he was shocked that being gay and an alcoholic, Jesus was unconditionally loving on him in such a powerful way.

Miracles Work by Love

For two years many LGBT friends and most of the downtown street population came to the REHOP and Burning Spokane. They testified to the non-judgmental acceptance, love and friendliness they encountered from everyone! We opened the microphone for anyone to sing and share from their hearts. No one was judged and everyone was embraced with heartfelt love. We didn't preach the gospel, as much as we sang it. God wanted to sing to people, not preach at them. No one was experiencing an unhealthy fear of God. Anyone who came to the front for a touch from God experienced one. God wasn't excluding anyone, no matter what their pain and behaviors were like. Jesus came to heal the brokenhearted and to set the captives free. He didn't come to condemn but to save and seek that which was lost.

There were signs, wonders and miracles that took place. A crippled young gothic man who was confined to a wheelchair and living on the streets would sometimes come to our meetings. At one of these meetings we prayed for him and he was healed. He left his wheelchair behind and still walks to this day.

Heavenly gold sparkles began appearing on many people's hands in the parking lot one night. On another night, as the band was playing, a man came in who was very drunk on alcohol. Fine gold dust appeared all in his hair and scalp. He was unaware it was there. It was quite amazing! In the book of Acts it talks about unusual miracles that would happen in the inner cities through the disciples of Jesus. These gold dust miracles were like that. The reason gold appears is because gold in the Bible speaks of the rich splendor of God and His glory. It also speaks of our worth to Him. He gives us His gold for our ashes. He sees us as pure gold through Christ.

Some people who profess Jesus Christ can be judgmental and have hard hearts. During one of our REHOP gatherings, a group of men similar to the street preachers seen on the news with signs saying, "God hates Fags!" showed up. They began to film gays and alcoholics coming in and out of one of our meetings. They shouted that we were going to hell and that God's judgment was on us. They even put it online and publicly wrote that I was a flaming gay pastor. They had no idea who I was or anything about my story. And yes, I am flaming! I'm on fire for the Lord. I'm a L.over of G.od B.eing T.rue! That's why it was called, "Burning Spokane!" I was proud to have LGBT friends and others that were socially outcast attending. That's exactly who Jesus would have wanted there if it were His place. And it was His place!

The power of the gospel, the spiritual music, light shows, food, clothing and tons of love impacted downtown Spokane! This lasted for two years until the building was sold, which ended that phenomenal Rainbow Electric love outreach.

Today as I walk the streets I still see many people who came to these meetings and still call me their pastor. They share how their lives have changed for the better since experiencing Jesus' love at the REHOP and Burning Spokane.

Chapter 14

The Cowardly Lion

New Courage Arises!

Dorothy meets the cowardly Lion on the Yellow Brick Road. He was the king of the forest but was scared of just about everything, even his own tail. He had to act strong, but was very timid inside from a spirit of fear.

Because I was bullied so much in my past, both at home and at school, I had a spirit of fear. Jesus is not only called the Lamb of God but also a Lion. Through His spirit I began to discover a new courage emerge when I encountered bullies.

The Lions Roar

In the mid 80's my pastor asked if I'd like to go to New York City to be part of a national inner city street evangelism campaign. I went to learn how to open-air preach on the streets in downtown Manhattan with other zealous soul-winning street preachers from all over the nation. It was an incredible experience. We had every kind of street preaching you could imagine with many diverse personalities. We had drama teams performing gospel skits on the streets as well. I did a mime depicting a person who killed himself with a fake gun dramatizing an addicted man who was suicidal. As I was lying on the sidewalk in front of a porn shop on 42nd Street, a little crowd gathered to see what happened. While they were watching me on the ground, the porn shop attendant came out and began to kick me. It wasn't good for his business. This reminded me of the nuns who stood in front of a porn shop in the movie *Sister Act*.

Someone on our team began to talk to the crowd as I lay there on the sidewalk, seemingly dead, asking them if they would go to heaven or hell when they die. They talked about the love of God and His free gift of salvation and the forgiveness of sins through Jesus Christ. I learned different ways of communicating the gospel there. I was also handed a megaphone to preach the gospel for my first time. This was very scary for me to do in the crowd on 42nd Street. I stepped out, opened my mouth and preached the gospel. People stopped to listen on every street corner. It was as though they were mesmerized. I was amazed how many people stopped to listen. I wasn't yelling at the people about God. I was just proclaiming the good news of Jesus the best I knew how. I had never done that before and it took great courage for me to do so.

When I came back to Spokane I had such zeal to preach the gospel in the open-air with a megaphone on a downtown street corner. My pastor, along with other pastors and some church members, joined me for this new exciting evangelistic campaign. They came with me for a few weekends and then discontinued after the newness began to wear thin. I continued because of the need for people to hear the message. A new group of street preachers began to join me, some being quite judgmental. They told me they were prophets and believed we were in God's end-time judgment. I was more into God's end-time love.

Eight years later while in St. Ives, Cornwall, England, while co-leading a mission trip, a lady on our team introduced herself to me and shared she had been cruising the strip with her girlfriends and had given her life to Jesus when I was open-air preaching in Spokane. She was full of gratitude and joy in her new exciting life in Christ because of that. I didn't know that my megaphone preaching had much effect, if any at all. That was really not my style but God can and will use anything.

The Pride Lion Parades

Some years ago I led a small musical parade in the idyllic artist and fisherman community of Saint Ives, Cornwall in England. We stayed in a beautiful, gardened mansion. I had brought costumes to wear for creative outreach. I led and organized a musical-dance parade through the downtown cobblestone streets in this coastal town. We would stand in the city square and one by one someone from our team in a costume would step out before the people and sing a song about God and His love. The rest of the team had percussion instruments and would join in. We had a police escort and the people of the town said they had not seen anything like it. I led another musical parade through the streets of downtown Nairobi, Kenya as well. The last parade I had seen there was a political protest between the old and the new president. Those parades seemed dark and fearful but mine were joyous and peaceful. It took courage to do these things in foreign lands.

The Martyr's Crown and the Spokane City Gate Street Church

One evening in 1986 as I was open-air preaching in Spokane, a few self-styled young satanist kids started burning Bibles near me and began to chant "Hail satan!" I decided to continue preaching the good news boldly. I wasn't mean spirited or obnoxious, I just preached that Jesus came to free us from the power of satan, forgive all our sins and that He was the Lord and Savior. I did preach that there was a heaven and a hell and that people could choose Jesus or satan. There is no in-between...you are either on one side or the other. You are either for Jesus or against Him. It was pretty direct and bold and also my first time to ever do this. It was risky and scary but I felt I was making a spiritual difference to anyone that heard the gospel that night.

A little riot broke out between the devil people and the Christians. It was interesting to say the least and the police came. Then a bully street gang leader came to me and threatened me. He said if I were to come back to that street corner the next weekend, he would smash my head open. I believed him. He didn't look or sound like he was playing games.

I was the cowardly lion. I had a spirit of fear and was afraid of being hurt, but my experience with God and my understanding of His reality outweighed the threat. I knew my message of Jesus Christ and His salvation for lost souls was true and worth dying for. I'm sure I was an enigma to many Christians and people. Here I was, a former flaming gay guy now preaching the gospel of Jesus Christ with a lion's courage before ranting satanists and bullies. Wow! I was surprised myself. What Jesus did for me on the cross by being tortured and forgiving of His enemies was way beyond any suffering I could imagine to save lost and angry humanity. What He did He also commanded us to do, which is to preach the good news to all creation. Jesus also said we would be persecuted for His name's sake. There's a scripture that says, "Do not be afraid of them when they oppose you for it will be a sign to them that you will be saved and they will be destroyed." (Philippians 1;28) God's word, through Paul, goes on to say that in the moment of attack God's presence will rest upon you.

That week I called my pastor Jim, who is one of the most gracious and genuine people I have ever known. To this day he is a great friend and mentor. I told him of the threat and I really didn't know what to do. Not only was I asking him but I was asking myself "should I take my stand for Christ and possibly have my head bashed in, maybe even die, or should I just not go back to that corner the following weekend?" I had to dig deep within myself to decide how real Jesus and His gospel was to me. Was it worth being wounded or possibly die for? It would have been easier to just not show up. Paul the Apostle talked about being sheep led to slaughter for the testimony of Jesus because of the persecution from his enemies. I was about to find out a little bit of what that kind of Christian experience would be like.

I'd been going faithfully every weekend preaching the gospel open-air at that same location. Hundreds of young people were cruising by partying in their cars to show off. There was a lot of excitement at that street corner and it was the hot spot in the city on weekends. My pastor talked to me about what the Bible calls, The Martyr's Crown. He told me he wasn't telling me to go or not to go, but if I did I would be choosing to possibly die for Christ. I had to pray all week and even fasted without food. This was not a game and it was a difficult choice for me to make. I had to face my greatest fears. I prayed through and made the choice. I wasn't going to be a coward anymore. I wanted Jesus to be proud of me for letting His love be greater than anything the world could offer.

I showed up the next weekend. I preached more boldly than I had before and sure enough the bully showed up. He had a small company of friends and homies with him to watch him smash my head open. He was going to show them how great and powerful he was. He believed that fear was more powerful than love. I had to prove something else. Satan holds people as slaves through fear, but God's love poured into us, by the power of the Holy Spirit, casts out all fear. Darkness fades and runs from light. We are the light of the world.

The bully came at me with a glass ashtray in his hand and asked if I was going to run to the police. I stood there eye to eye with him and silently asked the Lord to save this man and asked that His love would flow out of me and into his heart. As I did that I could feel God's love and forgiveness flow out to this man.

I Died, Without Dying

As he swung the ashtray toward my head, his arm suddenly stopped just at my hairline and he backed away saying, "Dude, you're weird!" He just walked away. That was it. I prepared for the worst. I did it...I didn't run. His friends were sitting around me on a concrete ledge waiting and wanting to see blood. And they did. They saw the blood of Jesus in action. They saw me forgive and love him. They saw my message of the good news of Jesus Christ wasn't a game, nor was it a show with a megaphone to impress people. I was more of a man in that moment than I ever thought I could be. In fact, I was a courageous lion!

As a result of my courage to stand for Christ, my pastor gathered other pastors in the city for the purpose of purchasing a building for the people on the streets. They called it the City Gate and they found a new street pastor to lead the work. The City Gate Street Church has become one of the city's leading outreaches for the homeless and street community. I just thank God for the wonderful ongoing fruit that has been sustained there because God helped me to overcome fear.

Gay Prostitution, Supernatural Healing and Jail

God's courage didn't stop there but continued to work in and through me. A lady who was a leader of a Women's Aglow chapter in San Francisco wanted to go with me and my friend Grace to the gay prostitution strip on Polk Street. This was a place that had been part of my past. She wanted to experience a divine guidance outreach for the purpose of reaching out to gay sex workers. I was very happy to try this out and to lead the way. As we were driving down Polk street, I parked near a gay dance club where some guys were looking for tricks. Parking my car, I was trying to think of a way to break the ice with these guys and an idea suddenly came to mind. I jumped on top of my car which they didn't know was ours because we had walked around the block. To them it appeared as though I jumped on someone else's car. I pulled up my pant leg to oncoming traffic as though I were aggressively trying to pull a trick. This brought hilarious shock to them and they all started laughing. They instantly liked me!

We began to talk and I asked them if they wanted me to sing something on my guitar. They said yes. As they gathered around, I opened the trunk of my car to retrieve the guitar and a young Latino guy saw I had a blue, silver and gold threaded dance outfit which I used for worship dance presentations in the trunk, as well. He asked if he could put it on over his clothes and try it out. I let him and off he went, twirling around, showing it to everyone around him. Unbeknownst to him, I now had a worship dancer performing while I sang songs about God. As I was singing, one of the guys who dropped the F bomb in every sentence suddenly yelled out, "It's healed! It's healed!" He started to apologize to us for his foul language and began to share with us and his friends that all the pain left his broken finger that was in a cast. He was experiencing the presence of God while I was singing and his friend was twirling about in a worship garment. We became friends instantly and ended up praying for all of them to receive Jesus, which they did. It was amazing.

Grace and I felt led to invite this young man, named Jay, to leave San Francisco with us since he had no family or job. He was very happy to join us and we took him to Disneyland where we had the most wonderful time. Jay also received the baptism of the Holy Spirit with the gift of tongues causing him to be filled with a new spiritual peace, joy and love that he had never felt before. We then asked if he would like to go with us to Tacoma and we'd help him get set up in his own apartment. The trip back was filled with laughter, conversation and singing. It was truly a joy-filled time. Jay shared with us that he had HIV. He told us that the pain he was experiencing due to his HIV effects had left his body. His heart was being healed just like his body was being healed.

We got him settled in an apartment and soon had to leave for a couple weeks for a ministry appointment. We connected him with friends that would help him grow in his new found faith. He said he would be fine while we were gone and was looking forward to our return.

When we returned we stopped by his apartment. Jay was there. We heard him inside but he wouldn't answer the door. We kept knocking until he emphatically told us to go away. We were dismayed. Our friendship was a beautiful one. God touched him, saved him and filled him with His spirit through us. We had taken him to Disneyland and brought joy and hope for a new future for him. For some reason he was completely blowing it all off. I was wondering what we could do to win his heart back. A thought came to my mind. Grace and I began to sing some of the sweet songs that the three of us sang together on our road trip. We wanted Jay to remember the love and joy we shared together. Instead of opening the door and being gracious to us, he told us that if we didn't stop and leave, he was going to call the police. We were shocked.

We were praying for wisdom for his soul because we knew he was turning his back on everything. The Spirit of God brought us to Jay to give him a special gift from God...a hope and a future in Christ. We had done nothing to hurt, control or use him, like so many others had done. That's all Jay had known from others. We were giving him something different with no strings attached. We began to think of what Jesus would do. We thought about Jesus suffering on the cross by the very people He was sent to, so we decided to demonstrate a little of that to Jay. We continued to sing songs through the door until the police came. We didn't resist arrest but we didn't walk with them either. We wanted the arrest to be a little dramatic for Jay's sake, so that he could see his friend and a kind lady, who was like a mother to him, being carried and dragged down the stairs because of his attitude. We were taken to jail. We knew we would go. But we did it to show Jay that we were willing to go to jail for him. He had nothing to give us and it would have been so easy for us to let him go because he was a rather high maintenance individual.

I was put in a waiting tank jail cell with Bloods and Crypts gang members from the Tacoma Hill Top area. I was the only white guy in the cell. I felt a little bit nervous but there wasn't much I could do. We were all waiting to go before the judge to get our sentences. Before any of us were called in, I felt God's spirit drop on me like a blanket of power. He revealed to me that he wanted me to stand up, share why I was there and to tell them that if they'd let me pray for them God would do something special for them before the judge.

I was very nervous to say the least. I was thinking, what happens if I stand up boldly before these hardened gang members, preach to them and nothing happens? It was scary. But a courage came into this cowardly lion that was not of me. This cowardly lion had to obey and cooperate with Jesus, the Lion of Judah! I took a deep breath and decided to trust God, like I had been learning to do. I shared with them that I was arrested for singing, even though my voice wasn't that bad. They all began to laugh. I then shared with them some of my story in Christ. As I was boldly talking I got an insight from the Holy Spirit. I said, "All of you know God on one level or another. You've all been to church but aren't walking the path of Christ. You're prodigals." They looked at me in shock but many of their heads were nodding in conviction because they knew it to be true. I then told them that if they'd allow me to pray for them, that God would do something special for them. It got really quiet. I was standing up telling them that if they'd do what I said, then God would do something for them. That was bold and courageous to say the least! I couldn't believe this was happening.

One of the obvious leaders quite loudly shouted, "Pray!" They all bowed their heads. I began to pray for them, for their souls and for their return to God. I thanked God that he was going to do something through the judge for them, since Jesus was the ultimate judge and is able to change the decisions of natural judges. Miracles now needed to happen, for my sake and for theirs!

One by one these scary dudes went before the judge. When the first one came back to our holding cell, I asked him publicly what happened. He told us that the judge let him go on personal recognizance. I then said out loud, "Can you thank Jesus for that in front of us all?" He agreed, thanking Jesus, so that everyone could hear. Then the next one went, the next one and the next. Everyone of them got the exact same release from the judge except for two. There were about twenty men there. The two that didn't, weren't finished with the judge. God had something good for them as well; we just didn't know at the time. Everyone of them gave thanks to Jesus in front of their peers in the jail cell. It was amazing and we were all having church!!!!

Then it was my turn. I was nervous and wondering if I would get out. To my joy I also got released like the others. My friend Grace, who is twenty years older and who has never been to jail or broken the law, was in a another cell with women. Even though we had both decided to do this for the Lord and for Jay, I was very concerned for her. Grace was released as well. After our release we approached Jay again. A similar thing happened. We were called into court sometime later from Jay pressing charges but he didn't show up. The judge told Grace and I that he saw we were good and kind people and he wouldn't be surprised if he saw us again because of our willing demonstration of love for Jay. He stated that this Jay guy was worthless and we should not waste our time and should just go our way.

What the judge didn't know was that I had also been a gay prostitute in San Francisco and other places. I had HIV and was a basic loser in life. To others I was considered worthless but I discovered that God sent His son Jesus to die on the cross. He knew sinners were victims of the darkness of this world and He came to save, heal and restore us to our divine worth. The Bible says that before the world was formed, He knew us and created us for good works planned in advance! Jesus came for sinners. He turns gays to saints, and LGBT's to L.overs of G.od B.eing T.rue. He shed his blood for Bloods, and rose from the crypt for Crypts!

We never saw Jay again but we did see an article in the paper that a cult group was arrested in an apartment building hallway. OMG, that was us! If singing, healing, renting an apartment for a lost young man, and going to jail for him is a cult, then Jesus must have been a cult leader. And there were those people who thought He was, yet He came to love and seek out those who were lost.

Chapter 15

Fireballs!

The Religious Witch threw fireballs at Dorothy's friend

Dorothy has persevered in the warfare against her new identity in the spiritual kingdom of Oz. It has taken heaven-sent friends helping her along the way–friends who have the heart of God, the mind of Christ and great courage. In the movie, *The Wizard of Oz*, the witch threw fireballs at the Scarecrow, one of Dorothy's new best friends.[1]

In 1991, God sent me one of these true friends. Her name is Grace. Before she entered my life I had been given a prophetic word from my pastor. He told me God was going to send someone to aid me in my journey on the Yellow Brick Road. He didn't use that terminology but told me she and I would not be married and she would have the special skills that I would need. He also shared that she would be a very loyal friend.

Within a few months of that word, Grace, who I had only known as an acquaintance from a church I attended, began showing up at my meetings. For three months she drove two hours each night to support me in any way that was needed. I did not ask her to help me, nor did anyone else for that matter. She just came.

Grace did not tell me at the time she was going to school because her husband was wanting a divorce. He divorced her and

---

1 (LeRoy & Fleming, 1939)

soon after he remarried. She had been a wife and mother for 25 years, as well as an assistant in her husband's dental office. She had also been a school teacher and a volunteer worker for various international Christian ministries and was now getting further education to go out into the workplace.

One day while Grace was taking a class, God spoke to her and told her to quit school to help me with my meetings for three months. She shared with me that God had put the LGBT community deeply on her heart while she was visiting San Francisco. She began to cry out that God would do something special for this community to help them know His amazing heart of love for them. Grace had never been involved with the LGBT community before this time. Little did she know that God would connect her with Dorothy's Club, starting with me in Corvallis, Oregon.

Grace moved with me to Seattle and we started a L.ove G.od B.e T.rue church in the middle of Capitol Hill, the LGBT district, in our apartment on Boylston Avenue. We held two to three gatherings every week. LGBT people would come, have dinner, worship with us and have encounters from God. I would say that most of them had authentic encounters with the power of God. Many of them began to prophesy and see visions. This became our normal. It was beyond amazing to see God's spirit touch the lives of those who came to our home church!

Grace began to be rejected by many of the close people in her life. For years she had served with a couple of international ministries and had donated much money to them as well. She was "fireballed" by them and experienced horrible character assassination. Many of them even went so far as to say that her working with me was an appearance of evil.

Most of what Jesus did according to the religious leaders of His day was an appearance of evil as well. He ate and drank with sinners and they called Him a drunkard and a glutton! They accused Him of being a demon and also said the power that came through Him wasn't of God but from the devil. He was a close friend to adulterers, the demon possessed, a despised Samaritan woman, harlots and lepers. Jesus would have been wonderfully loved by the LGBT community but I'm sure the religious leaders would have called Him a Fag and a compromiser. I was called a flaming homosexual and cursed to hell on a website and Youtube video by loser hate preachers at a conference I held downtown Spokane that was for the purpose of helping people to care for and to build bridges with the LGBT community in God's love. I used to be a flaming homosexual, but now I'm a completed LGBT—a L.over of G.od B.eing T.rue on flames of fire in the Spirit of God! Jesus loved the broken, stigmatized and outcast people then, and He still loves them today. He was so full of love and compassion that He gave up His reputation and desires His people to do the same. This is what it meant when Jesus said to take up your cross daily and to follow Him. Taking up your cross actually means to suffer character assassination and a ruined reputation by people who judge outwardly and who don't see the intentions of the heart. To God, that is a true appearance of evil. More than that, it is actually a form of evil, which God's people are admonished to abstain from. Self righteous based religion outside of trusting and believing faith in God's power for miracles and transformation, is associated with witchcraft, according to the book of Galatians.

> *Oh foolish Galatians, who hath bewitched you, that ye should not obey the truth, before whose eyes Jesus Christ hath been evidently set forth, crucified among you, Received ye the Spirit by the works of the law or by the hearing of faith? Are ye so foolish? Having begun in the Spirit, are ye now made perfect in the flesh. Have ye suffered so many things In vain? If it be yet In vain. He therefore that ministers to you the Spirit, and worketh miracles among you, doeth he it by the works of the law, or by the hearing of faith?*
> *Galatians 3:1-5 KJV*

Grace still continues with me to this day and is loved by so many in the LGBT community. She has suffered the loss of many who were near and dear to her heart. When she joined me in the ministry of the love of God, and the grace of Jesus Christ, she bore the stigma of LGBT and of those living and dying with HIV and AIDS. She was rejected and "fireballed" by many of her closest friends and family. The fire of religion was thrown at Grace, trying to keep her from helping Dorothy free the land of Oz. They were also aimed at thwarting her ministry to those in desperate need to receive hope, honor and a sense of dignity. One of the greatest scriptures that reminds me of Grace is:

> *There is no greater love than one lay down their lives for their friends.*
> *John 15:13*

Chapter 16

Poppies, Witchcraft and Snow

The Witch put a spell on Dorothy, her heart, mind
and courage through opiates...poppies
Which are pleasing to the eye and the smell.

There were times in my journey that I was lured away and put to sleep by poppies. Opium is made from poppy seeds. The street drug called meth, an opiate, was a very powerful drug of choice I had used coupled with sexual experiences in the early 80's. It was very addictive. If you get free at one point and try it again later, it makes it so much harder to get free from it again. The witch will use anything with an agenda to disarm us in the battle as we walk in our ruby slippers. After Dorothy's time of sleeping in the poppy field, the Holy Spirit released snow upon her to wake her up so she could continue her journey of transformation.

Sin Didn't Separate Me from Glinda

If I make my bed in hell, you are there.
Psalm 139:8

I'm going to share a few experiences where I was put to sleep by poppies. This basically means I was relapsing into former sexual and drug behaviors.

On one occasion I was feeling very discouraged and disheartened. I was in a gay cruising park on meth looking for a sexual hookup. As I was walking through this park, the snow of divine revelation from God fell upon me.

Suddenly in the middle of the park I received a downpour of supernatural euphoria and love. It was similar to experiences I had before yet extraordinarily unique and intimate from God. I was stunned. This was pure love and it was beyond the "high" I was experiencing in this particular moment. A drug high isn't real love, it's chemically induced euphoria. There's a difference. I asked God, "Why are you doing this? I don't deserve it! I'm high on meth and I'm going to engage in some sexual behavior in this park." I also told Him I was still going to go through with my plans, even though deep in my heart I didn't want to. It was hurting me very much to think I would still do something that would offend God especially after having a divine encounter with His love in such an incredible way. He spoke to me and said, "I know you are. I'm doing this because you are My son. I love you very much. You are not a disappointment to Me and I know what you're going through. You have a good heart and I know that you love Me. I'm giving you a divine hug right now so when you turn back to Me you don't have to come to Me in shame and fear. I am demonstrating My love right now to cast out your fear of returning back to Me. I love you just as much when you fall as when you're doing well. You mean so much to Me. I love you more than you can imagine." This personal word spoken to me was the snow that God used to wake me up helping me return to the path of God's purpose for my life.

The witch didn't like God intervening in the poppy field where she had lured me. Why did I go back to these former behaviors when God had been so good to me over the years? There were unhealed parts of my heart, unmet needs and unresolved offenses that I still had. No one was at fault for my choices and God has always been good to me. I was reacting as I had when younger coping with the stress and anger. I had totally given my heart and my life to Jesus and His work. I had never had counseling or any real therapeutic help for my psychological and emotional needs. These relapses caused me to realize that I wasn't whole as a person just because I was a follower of Christ. I needed help. Going to church, listening to sermons, serving and having healthy relationships, wasn't enough for me. I needed professional help for the deep-seeded issues embedded in my heart from child-hood.

Amazing Grace

In this relapse stage I went into an adult book store. I was on meth again and in a private booth watching a porn movie. I was crying from the pain of being away from my God who had loved me so much. I was feeling so degraded, ashamed and depressed. The snow came upon me once again. The song "Amazing Grace" began to play from the movie machine. It broke me and I began to sob. God broke the spell in my mind by reminding me of His amazing grace that saved a wretch like me and continues to save me.

Instead of causing me to be afraid of Him during my failings, He allowed His snow to fall fresh on me. The Bible says that God's kindness leads us to turn around. It also says that His per-fect love casts out all fear. Glinda, the Holy Spirit of God, rained mercy and grace upon me over and over again as many times as I needed, to truly awaken me to His love and be willing to let go of the idols of false intimacy and comfort. God was power-fully showing me that His love reaches to the deepest places of my heart. It would have been hard for me to believe if I had not experienced it more than once. One of my favorite scriptures is in Psalm 139 where it says that "if I make my bed in hell, He is there." (Psalm 139:8) Another one also says that darkness and light are the same to the Lord. I could make my bed in darkness, but God's eyes of love and favor would remain upon me and He would reach out His hand to me to help me wake up and to rise and walk. His mercies are new every morning, great is His faithfulness! He sees me as His child that He is proud of and never as an enemy He's ashamed of. That is how He sees everyone that accepts Jesus. King David in the Bible was called "a man after God's own heart." He was a king who committed murder and adultery and who made many mistakes but continued to put his trust in the mercy of God, despite his frailties. He sought God for help in his times of distress. He experienced consequences for his actions, as I have also, but God always lifted up his head and continued to give him hope for the future.

A Snow Prophecy from Glinda

Snow represents the living word of God that comes to us to cleanse us, like fresh falling snow, and to wake us up from our dream state induced by opiates, illusions, and addictions.

During this two year relapse season in the poppies, I attended a Christian conference. The speaker was well known. Suddenly in the middle of his message he said there was a man in the congregation struggling with meth. It was me. He told me that God showed him that I was at a baseline in my heart. He also began to talk about suicide. He said God didn't want him to point me out but to give me a message. He then said without looking at me that Jesus wanted him to tell me how much He loved me and He had a special heart of love for people caught in addictions. This speaker had a great reputation for prophetic accuracy. I was the only one aware that this was absolutely for me.

I was preparing to leave for Las Vegas on a business trip and I wasn't sure I would make it back. I was falling under the witch's spell to destroy my life and to forfeit my ruby slippers. I felt I wasn't able to rise up at this point unless God did something to intervene. I felt so much shame and discouragement and felt I was losing my heart, my mind and my courage.

God used this amazing man, named Shawn, to awaken my heart with the fresh snow of His living word to me. It astounds me to see how God has pursued me and shown His love to me over the years. It would have been so easy to give up on life. It has been very humiliating over the years to go through what I have struggled with and to be open and honest with others about it. Even in writing this book I have had to pray to for the strength to be vulnerable and courage to proclaim this message. But I want to kick some witch butt by turning my scars into stars. I also want to turn my mess into a message and all the tests into testimonies about our amazing God and His Son Jesus Christ, my Lord and Savior.

Party and Pray

I met some gay men who were having a sex and drug gathering in their home. They called it "Party and Play." This is a term used by gay culture that represents sex and drugs, especially meth and other euphoric poppy-drugs. Because I was feeling unable to get out of this poppy patch and this spell, I allowed myself to mix some of these drugs. I wasn't engaging sexually with anyone at this party and was sitting alone in a bedroom. I felt myself starting to slip into unconsciousness. Just as I hit the baseline, as that speaker had foretold, the snow from Glinda came upon me again. I could have died or ended up going to the hospital from an overdose. Who knows? I was weary from the battle of life. I didn't want to die, but I also didn't want to continue in this way.

The Voice of the Snow

I heard the gentle voice of God in my spirit say very clearly, "Do you love Grace?" God was talking about my dearest friend. This person Grace who believed in me, walked with me and helped me for so many years. This amazing woman had given up so much and truly believed God sent her to me for a divine purpose of destiny. I had never had a friend like Grace and I couldn't imagine my life without someone like her. Glinda was using her as leverage to wake me up and to get me back on my feet again. When I heard this I knew God was working on my heart. I felt as though I were having a "spiritual heart attack" that could have possibly led to a real heart attack. I knew He was asking me if my dearest friend Grace was worth living for. There was so much behind that. Of course she was, although I felt I had let her down too much. She had walked with me and was proud that I had been so courageous.

God then began to ask me the same questions regarding other people in my life who mattered to me. As God began to speak to me about being willing to live for others outside of myself, I began to come out of the drug-induced stupor. I went outside on the porch and started talking to God. I said, "OK, You have me back but is there any hope for me?" Right after I asked this I looked up into the early evening sky and saw a rainbow suddenly begin to appear. It wasn't a normal rainbow arc that we normally see. It appeared like a plant coming out from the ground rising to the sky and became like a blossoming flower. God gave me a rainbow flower as a sign of His love and promise. "Party and Play" became "Party and Pray."

I have heard many times how sin separates us from God. It separates us because it breaks off the sweet fellowship of His presence. I learned through many different situations that it didn't separate His relationship with me. He still saw me as His Dorothy, His angel, His chosen baby. His love empowers me; it does not enable my bad behaviors.

The word of God also declares that even when we are faithless, He is always faithful! God showed me that in my darkness He loved me just as much as when I was walking in the light.

It's like getting F's on a report card but God only sees A's. Jesus is the A on my report card. It's not by works, but by faith that God is pleased with us. God is proud of me because I believe in

His mercy and unfailing love. I don't give up. Like the righteous, though I fall many times, I rise again! Not rising up in God's mercy and love is the worst failure of all.

Snow Promises

Rejoice not against me, O my enemy. Though I have fallen, I shall rise. Though I dwell in darkness, the Lord is my Light!
Micah 7:8

Where can I flee from your Presence? If I ascend to heaven, You are there; if I make my bed in hell, you are there!
Psalm 139:7-8

Come, let us reason together says the Lord, though your sins be as scarlet, I shall make them like fresh fallen snow!
Isaiah 1:18

Chapter 17

The Emerald City

The Emerald City and the Horse of a Different Color

*But God has selected for His purpose the foolish
things of the world to shame the wise revealing their
ignorance, and God has selected for His purpose the
weak things of the world to shame the things which are
strong revealing their frailty. God has selected for His
purpose the insignificant (base) things of the world, the
branded, and the things that are despised and treated
with contempt, even the things that are nothing, so that
He might reduce to nothing the things that are.*

1 Corinthians 1:27-28 Amplified Bible (AMP)

"Who Rang That Bell?"

Dorothy and her friends finally arrive at the Emerald City and
ring the doorbell. A guardian leans out of an upper window looking down on them asking "Who rang that bell?"

After a short dialogue he brushes them off and tells them that
no one can see the great Oz. When they inform him that Dorothy is wearing the ruby slippers of divine election, the guardian
totally changes his tune responding, "Well that's a horse of a different color, come on in!"

For many years I have been closely associated to charismatic Christianity, which I call the Merry Ol' land of Oz. For the majority of that time I have felt like a horse of a different color.

I believed clergy leaders held the keys for me to gain the knowledge and experience for the maturing necessary in the supernatural kingdom of Jesus Christ, which they did to a large degree.

I felt many times that the "guardians" looked down on me because I was *a horse of a different color*. I wasn't the same color as the others who were in the churches where I participated. There were many times my fellow brothers and sisters in Christ would label me strange, weird and out of the box.

It was true! Jesus picked me straight out of a gay rainbow parade and gave me my ruby slippers. I was His chosen baby! Once again I began to wonder if the "chosen baby" thing was going to be similar to my past experience in being treated as the "unwanted baby."

A pastor gave me my new "chosen baby" book called "the Bible." There were many promises of hope, a future, acceptance, favor, love and unity in family. There was even a promise in this book that God would do exceedingly above anything that I could ever ask or imagine. Because of my supernatural encounter at the parade, it was my invitation to believe again that I had value and worth–that I meant something to people and to God. I was granted a new birth with a new family and with a new promise. I would have to persevere through this new promise with a new faith, even though my fears were still intact. I couldn't help but wonder if I would experience stigmatization by my new spiritual family members.

Because of my gay background, which was evident to any church community I sought to be a part of, I entered without much celebration. It felt more like toleration. When they saw I had the tangible evidence of the Holy Spirit working in my life, being my ruby slippers in action, I became more acceptable.

There was a time I heard God speak to me that I would be staying in what's called the Timothy House in Spanish Harlem. It was supervised by a famous church which was founded by David Wilkerson who wrote the book, *The Cross and the Switchblade*. He also founded Teen Challenge which is worldwide and helps people struggling with different kinds of addictions.

I had been reading one of David Wilkerson's newsletters I received on a monthly basis. I loved his messages. His newsletters really challenged me to give my all to the maturity and calling that God calls each of us to. As I was looking at a picture of this discipleship house he had founded, the Spirit clearly revealed to me I would be going there and ministering in different ways. Living in Spokane at the time, I was instructed by the Spirit to call and ask if they would host me for a couple of weeks. This direction from God was so real that I immediately picked up the phone and "knocked at the door of that Emerald City community." I asked them if they hosted guest ministers and they said that they sometimes do. I then asked them if I could come. They said no. An hour later the Lord instructed me to call again. I felt very awkward calling and "knocking" again, but I did. When I asked the same question, once again I was told no. I was really embarrassed. The guardian at the door was not letting me in. Then the Lord told me to call one more time and share with them about my encounter at the gay pride parade. I was basically showing them my ruby slippers of election from God Himself. I took a really deep breath and called for the third time. This time I shared my story and was told yes. The door opened to their community.

I flew to New York staying at the Timothy House for two weeks. I would preach in their chapel and was allowed to participate in any of their outreach ministries. I was very interested in their Raven Truck homeless ministry. We would feed and minister to the homeless people living on the streets in cardboard boxes. I was also interested in their Crack Alley Ministry. I also attended their Sunday church meetings in the famous Mark Hellinger Broadway Theatre. That is where the original 1970's *Jesus Christ Superstar* was originally performed.

Even though they allowed me to join them in these ministries, I didn't feel very welcomed, though that feeling wasn't coming from David Wilkerson. He was one of my greatest inspirations. His street ministry staff wasn't too sure about me and followed me with a critical eye.

There was one incident where I went to Crack Alley and sat down by a gay gothic young man. He seemed lifeless, lost and completely alone. My heart went out to him as I saw him sitting alone. I sat down next to him and introduced myself and began to listen to the hardcore Bible preaching being presented. There was also a music-worship team playing songs for people to sing along. This man was not engaging at all. I asked if it would be OK for me to give him a hug and he agreed. I hugged him warmly and because of that, he opened his heart to God and lifted his hands with me. We both then stood together in praise and worship. That warm touch caused his heart to open to Jesus.

I then received the "shoulder tap" by one of the guardians, something I had become so accustomed to. I was asked to follow him and knew what was about to happen. I was then told that people who attended there did not need hugs, they needed to hear the Bible. I was then invited to leave. I noticed that my gay gothic friend lost heart when he perceived what was happening. He sat down and went back to his disengaged demeanor he had had before.

Later, in another street ministry experience, I prayed with a Mexican man to receive Jesus and to get the baptism of the Holy Spirit. He began to speak in a heavenly prayer language. I had to have someone interpret for me because he spoke in very broken English. The next day he found me at the church and shared with me, in full English, that he had a visitation from angels during the night. He told me that God had sent them to him and he had a powerful encounter with God. He said that it gave him the ability to speak English! It was a sign, a wonder and quite miraculous!

These leaders following me around were not happy that I had come and was ministering in this kind of way. I sensed they had a hard time believing that someone coming out of the gay world could minister like Jesus. Jesus operated with signs, wonders and miracles and told His believers to do the same, emphasizing they would do even greater works. I just happen to believe it and the Holy Spirit works with me through my ruby slippers.

One night David Wilkerson gave a very powerful, convicting message and did an altar call for personal cleansing and commitment to God. I went up with the crowd. You can't just sit there and not go to the altar when he gives a message from God. I went forward pouring my heart out before God and was again tapped on the shoulder and taken to the back of the theatre. One of the guardians asked me why I had gone forward. I responded that David Wilkerson had just preached. How could I not go forward? I was wondering why the guardians weren't up there! They viewed me in total judgment thinking I was living in sin yet wanting to be there as a minister. I had no desire to be a hypocrite. Being used of God never means that we don't have issues we need to deal with. Guardians should probably be at the altar more than anyone!

David Wilkerson pointed me out from the stage after the altar call that same Sunday morning. He did not know what had just happened and asked me "What I would like?" I was shocked. He was one of the greatest influences in my life and I saw him like a spiritual father. I never dreamed I would ever meet him and here he was asking me this question. I simply asked him for a father's blessing. I told him I lived in Spokane and followed his ministry through his newsletters and always wanted to meet him. He began to prophesy over me with his hands on my shoulders saying "You shall be a firebrand for God in America." David Wilkerson affirmed me. Some of his staff did not.

I was there because God opened a door and He was able to reach a gay gothic man through me from a small act of a hug.

Some of the guardians came and apologized at the end of my two week stay. They confessed they thought I was possibly a wolf in sheep's clothing. I was actually a "horse of a different color!"

The Ruby Slippers are the seal of the Holy Spirit and they cause doors "to open that no man can close and doors to close that no man can open!"
Revelations 3:7-8

Chapter 18

The Merry Old Land of Oz

In the Merry Ol' Land of Oz of Charismatic Christianity, all the
citizens are laughing the day away.

Dorothy, the horse of a different color, is welcomed into the
Emerald City only because of her ruby slippers. They provide
a carriage for Dorothy and her friends which is led by a horse
that changes colors. To me this magical horse represents what is
called the charismatic, supernaturally based, Christianity. Jesus
was the ultimate charismatic Christ. He taught His disciples how
to walk in the supernatural powers of God. He then poured out
the Holy Spirit on 120 disciples that had gathered together after
He was resurrected and they each received their ruby slippers.
These disciples appeared drunk or inebriated to many of the out-
siders who saw and heard them speaking in different languages.
What the onlookers soon learned was that they were under the
power of God because what they were hearing were the differing
languages from surrounding areas they each represented. Here is
Wikipedia's definition of charismatic Christianity:

> *Charismatic Christianity (also known as Spirit-filled*
> *Christianity) is a form of Christianity that emphasizes*
> *the work of the Holy Spirit, spiritual gifts, and modern-*
> *day miracles as an everyday part of a believer's life.*
> *Practitioners are often called Charismatic Christians or*

> *Renewal-ists. Although there is considerable overlap,*
> *charismatic Christianity is often categorized into three*
> *separate groups: Pentecostalism, the Charismatic*
> *Movement, and Neo-Charismatic Movement. According*
> *to the Pew Research Center, Pentecostals and*
> *Charismatic Christians numbered over 584 million or a*
> *quarter of the world's 2 billion Christians in 2011.*
> *(Wikipedia)*

I have to admit that I have experienced more joy, peace, love and laughter with charismatic Holy Spirit-filled Christians than any other people group. I believe laughter may be one of the greatest remedies for stress, depression and anxiety.

There is a proverb that states,

> *A merry heart does good like a medicine.*
> *Proverbs 17:22*

I can laugh like never before because I've been forgiven, cleansed and favored by God. This is all because of what Jesus accomplished on my behalf. I can't think of anything more helpful to me than to have a really fun time in life. It can be wearisome if Christianity is understood as "trying to be a better person and getting things 'straightened out.'" Living in and for God without a good amount of joy and laughter is like dry religion to me. The three main experiences of the kingdom of God are joy, righteousness and peace in the Holy Spirit. The Holy Spirit is like a fountain that springs out of our inner being. Jesus called the Holy Spirit new wine. He said that you cannot pour new wine into an old wineskin. The old wineskin represents powerless religion based on self effort. To mention old wineskin you have to assume there is a new one. This new wineskin is based on faith through the miraculous power of God. One of my favorite scriptures is in the metaphoric romance book in the Old Testament called Song of Solomon. It says, "He took me to the wine cellars and set His love in order within me." (Song of Solomon 2:4)

The L.overs of G.od B.eing T.rue can experience the intoxicating joy of His new wine. I have become more addicted to God's wine which has helped me exchange my addictions that brought empty satisfaction. God has brought me to His inner wine cellar and He has rewarded my diligence in seeking Him. I do my best to stay there, which Jesus called, "abiding." He said that He was the Wine Vine and we are the branches. One of my favorite books that explains how to do this is called *The Secret of the Stairs* by Wade Taylor.

Lonnie Frisbee, the Toronto Blessing and New Wine bringing Joy and Laughter!

Men prepare a meal for enjoyment, and wine makes life merry.
Ecclesiastes 10:9

I had mentioned Lonnie Frisbee in a previous chapter and wanted to honor him for truly following Jesus despite his struggles. I can relate so much with him and feel we could be twins. He was the young visionary hippie whose encounter with Jesus released the power of God that started the Calvary Chapel Jesus People Movement which then flowed into the charismatic movement with the Vineyard Church. Supernatural signs and wonders exploded. God chose Lonnie to be an amazing, crazy and fun power evangelist in reaching the world for Christ through his creative flamboyant personality along with the gifts of the Holy Spirit.

He struggled with homosexuality after being molested as a young boy, but not everyone has the propensity towards the gay lifestyle due to molestation. I believe many may be born with a genealogical predisposition. But Jesus tells us that through faith in Him we can have a rebirth and have a new genealogical disposition from God's DNA. We can then have a new orientation and can develop new identities, behaviors, habits and lifestyles.

A fresh renewing visitation of God's spirit came to a little airport Vineyard Church in Toronto, Canada. It became known as "The

Toronto Blessing." People came from all over the world to experience these incredible power encounters. I went to Toronto to see it for myself. It was mind blowing. No one was preaching. There was only worship music being played by a youth band. People would be standing in line outside to get in and they were getting zapped by God's power! No one was being prayed for. The happenings inside were as diverse as the people themselves. Some were laughing. Some were shaking and vibrating as though electricity was pulsating through them. Others were lying on the floor in complete tranquility! This went non-stop for some years!

One of the most outrageous things about this visitation from God was the uncontrollable laughter people were having. Although I didn't experience it for myself, it was quite a sight. I have never laughed so much in my life just by watching these encounters that these people were having. When I returned to Seattle this Holy Spirit phenomena had apparently transferred to me. As I traveled and hosted meetings in the Northwest this power began to touch others in a similar way.

I am learning so much about God on my journey and finding out just how much fun He is! I never would have equated fun and God together in the same sentence. He continues to surprise me with all He is and all He does. God has given me quite a sense of humor and an incredible imagination and has uniquely created each one of us with varying gifts and talents.

Angel and the Shooting Gallery at a Restaurant

I was one of the guest speakers, hosted by my wonderful friend and amazing man of God, Timothy Snodgrass, at a Glory Conference in Bend Oregon when the glory of God showed up. Everyone in this meeting was caught up in the pure joy of the atmosphere. Once again people were lying on the floor shaking, vibrating and laughing under the power of God. When the meeting was over we all staggered drunk in the spirit to a restaurant located across the street. This was not vodka...it was God-ka!

The glorious presence of God came with us. While people who had been at our conference were walking down the aisle of this restaurant going to their tables, I would simply point at them. Incredibly, everyone I pointed at would fall under the power of God in the aisles. None of the customers knew I was doing this, nor did they have a clue what was happening. I'm sure they were shocked. We were all just laughing so much and feeling quite tipsy, as though we had been drinking alcohol, but it was only the new wine of God's spirit. I would then walk down the aisle and point my finger at my friends who were sitting at a table while the waitress was taking orders. It was like God's arrows were striking them. Each one of them suddenly started flipping out and sliding down to the floor! No one could stop laughing and I wanted to get as much mileage out of this as I could. It was in a non-church atmosphere and was causing quite a scene. The poor waitresses! We did have opportunities to share with the people in the restaurant about the love and joy of God through Jesus Christ. There was no religion involved; it was only heaven's wine being poured out. The next day they had placed a notice on their door to keep whatever "it" was out of the restaurant! "It" was God and He gave people food and drink that was better than anything on that menu!

Kiss My Bass

I was given an animated singing bass plaque. The fish is rubbery and looks and feels like a real live bass. I took it to a local women's Christian gathering in Idaho Falls. After I gave my gospel message I told all the well dressed ladies to come to the front and line up, telling them they would have an encounter with God if they kissed my bass! This is just how crazy fun it was getting. I admit it was a bit over the top but I have discovered how God can and will flow out of our personalities. I told these ladies in the line to kiss the bass when he began to sing to them. His little fish head would bend forward facing you while singing *Take Me to the River and Don't Worry, Be Happy*. One by one, each lady reluctantly came face to face with this ugly singing bass and had to kiss it on the lips. When they did, each one of them had a supernatural laughing encounter. Some of them started rolling across the carpet laughing uncontrollably. If any of them had any kind of depression, worry or anxiety, it flew straight out the window and fast!

I used to think that being a Christian meant that you couldn't be yourself, especially if you had an out-of-the-box imagination. Like I said, I'm a horse of a different color. Someone once told me that the original dictionary definition of the word "weird" meant "belief in the supernatural and being out-of-the-box." Well if that's true, then I am weird…which then means that God is weird. I'm created in God's image! He uses weird people because He's out-of-the-box and extremely supernatural! I love it! I get to be me and have loads of fun with it in the Merry Ol' Land of Oz.

Hyatt Regency Lobby Holy Rollers

My friend Grace and I were attending a National Women's Christian Conference in Long Beach, California at a high end hotel. There were at least two thousand in attendance. As they began to pour out of the conference room I started to play my guitar and sing in the lobby. Women began to feel the presence of God and formed a circle around me. Many of the spectators, including the hotel staff, were watching and wondering what was taking place with all these interesting charismatics. As I began to spontane-ously sing and proclaim the joyous power of God, ladies began to dance in circles, many began to drop to the floor. These women were dressed to the hilt and were now rolling on the ground through the lobby in ecstatic laughter. A crowd gathered and watched this hysterical sight. I have heard there are very playful angels in heaven and they work in the glory realm of God's pres-ence through his ministers. I'm quite sure this is what was hap-pening. People were seeing that Christians can be some of the happiest and most fun people on earth! I have never experienced anyone or anything in this world having this kind of experience in joy and laughter. This came directly from the presence of God. We were demonstrating the GOOD news of Jesus Christ. He came to bring joy and laughter in place of mourning, depression and anxiety. God is funnier than the funniest comedian on earth. No one compares with Him!

Brian's Song

A friend asked me to meet her gay friend who lived in Capitol Hill, Seattle. I went to visit him and met his stepmother and her female partner. They seemed a bit closed towards me because my friend had told them I was a Christian, which I totally understood. When I met him, he was also wary of me because he thought I was going to put a guilt trip on him for his homosexuality. I had no reason to do that, nor did I want to. I put the ball in his court in deciding if he wanted to pursue any friendship. It was a slow process but the friendship did finally start to grow. He had received Jesus previously in his life and had been active as a missionary but there had been a lot of anger issues from his past causing a hardness of heart.

I also introduced him to my dear friend Grace and he really liked her. As Grace and I went to visit him one day we found him gasping for breath. He had pneumonia and was dying from AIDS. He then told us he had been given two weeks to live. I asked permission from his stepmom for Grace and I to go in and pray for him, if she thought he would be open to it. Everyone agreed. As we went to his bedside I felt overwhelmed with helplessness and asked God what to do. I simply began to quietly pray in my spirit language. After doing this for a couple of minutes something suddenly and powerfully happened which completely surprised us. He sat straight up and began to sing a message in tongues with a clear, strong voice. Immediately after he just sat there in this most serene state. His breathing totally changed and was now very soft and peaceful. We were stunned. As he sang his song in tongues during this encounter his stepmother came into the room and went to her knees before God. She knew he was having a spiritual experience with Jesus and was profoundly touched, as both Grace and I were. It was a very holy and beautiful moment. He then shared that he heard God speak to him. The Bible says that when you pray in tongues you can hear the interpretation of God's messages. This is what happened. He didn't just decide to pray in tongues. Truly, he could barely breathe. Rather, the power of God came on him and sang through him. It was incredible.

We were all crying during this experience while observing his special love encounter with Jesus. He stated that he felt he hadn't lived for God like he could have. He had served God in the past but had "fallen asleep in the poppies" like so many of us have done at times. The snow of God's presence woke him up, gave him new breath and restored his soul in a moment. He then asked us if we would share this at his funeral so Jesus would be glorified in front of his family and friends. We agreed. We shared that story at his funeral. His stepmom and her partner told Grace and I that we were the only Christians they felt best represented Jesus to them.

Playing with Dolls!

His stepmom then gave me a big black female doll which had belonged to him. She was about 2 feet long. I named her Sista' Petunia Joan.

The book of Acts and the New Testament records many unusual signs, wonders and miracles which took place. The Bible even goes so far as to say the world could not contain all the books written about the miracles Jesus did Himself! One unusual way the Spirit of God worked through the apostle Paul was people taking strips of cloth from him and laying them on those afflicted with various sicknesses and demonic oppression. They would be healed, saved and delivered.

I decided that if Paul could use cloth for Holy Spirit encounters then I could use a doll. I learned that God works through my unique personality and sense of humor. God is not stuffy, rigid or traditional. Even Jesus would do strange things like spit in dirt to make mud and place on someone's eyes to heal their blindness!

Sista Petunia Launches Glenn

When I had the L.ove G.od Be T.rue church in Seattle most people in our church were from the LGBT community and had received Jesus and were regularly having divine encounters. This was amazing! There was a young man named Glenn who wasn't gay but loved our church and our unconventional ways of ministry. He had a great sense of humor and really connected with us. He was really fun and we laughed a great deal. Today he has a miracle ministry where gemstones suddenly appear in meetings where he's speaking.

It was his birthday and we had a tradition to pray for a special encounter from God on birthdays. I asked him to stand in the center of the room so we could pray a blessing over him. He stood in the center with his arms crossed bracing himself so he wouldn't fall to the floor under the power of God. This was a very common occurrence at our home church. I asked God privately in my heart to do something different and show me what to do to bless him. A thought quickly came to my mind. Based on what flashed through my mind I grabbed the doll Petunia tapping his forehead with her cloth hand. We were all shocked with what happened next. Suddenly Glenn flipped upside down horizontally in the air and was shot across the living room and into the dining room by the power of God! God turned him into a human missile and fired away! He didn't get hurt but was totally knocked off his feet by this crazy birthday blessing. It was hysterical!

Sista Petunia and the Wave

I hosted and was a speaker at a conference in a Seattle hotel where I used Sista' Petunia. The creative spirit of God flowed through me and a thought came to me to use the doll again. So I picked her up and began speaking through her like a puppet. I then said to the people in my Sista' Petunia voice, "I wonder if you will all fall like dominos under the power of God if I do the wave?" I then took the Sista's hand and waved it. Sure enough the entire front row fell out in the Spirit on their chairs like dominos! It was outrageous and crazy. It was definitely out of the box.

Experiencing spiritual encounters can be the most fun, outrageous and creative encounters you could ever have or imagine! This isn't the only way God's power works but since one of the top three fruits of the Spirit is joy, this should be happening much more in believers' lives. Life can be way too serious. People can be way too serious. God works with people according to their views of Him and despite them as well. I just happen to believe in a joyful, fun heavenly Father who loves to play with His children. The older definition of the word gay used to mean happy and gleeful. God is gayer than we have ever imagined! When I come out of my prayer closet, I am fully gay, joyful and fun, just like God!

No matter who you are, or your personality style, God can use you and maximize your true self found in Christ.

Chapter 19

The Wonderful Wizard of Oz

Dorothy, even though she has proven the reality of God's work in her life through the storms, witches, poppies, lions and tigers and bears, she is still asked to prove herself. She seems to not be able to win, no matter what she does.

Dorothy and her friends are allowed to enter to see the Wizard of Oz. As they are walking down the ominous hallway they hear a loud booming voice cry out to come forward. As they walk into the cavernous room they see a huge image of a face. The voice and the scene creates great fear and awe causing Dorothy and her friends to tremble. Everyone, including Glinda, had called him "the wonderful Wizard of Oz" and gave the impression that he was kind and benevolent. This did not seem to be the case.

The great Oz thunderously declares that "I am the great and powerful Oz!"[1] He then proceeds to ask them who they are. Trembling, Dorothy tries to answer only to be interrupted by the Wizard telling them he already knows why they have come. He beckons the Tin Woodman forward and in a threatening tone confronts him as to why he dares to ask for a heart. The effeminate Tin Woodman, shaking uncontrollably, begins to share about their journey down the Yellow Brick Road when the Wizard cuts him off. He goes on to each friend and ends with the Cowardly Lion. He yells at the Lion who is falling apart at the seams and then faints.

---

1 (LeRoy & Fleming, 1939). In the book, Oz says ""I am Oz, the Great and Terrible. Why do you seek me?"

Dorothy steps up to the Wizard and confronts him. She courageously rises up with her heart and voice and says, "You ought to be ashamed of yourself! Frightening him like that when he came to you for help!" Once again the Wizard shouts to be silent proceeding to tell them they will have to prove themselves by performing a "very small task"...to bring back the broomstick of the Wicked Witch of the West. They suddenly realize they would have to kill her in order to take it and bring it back. However the Wizard is undaunted by his request. The Lion, who is scared to death, runs down the hallway and throws himself out the window.

The broomstick was a symbol of victory, sort of like Goliath's sword was a symbol of David's victory in battle. For me I have also been on a quest for victory that connected to fulfillment of God's call and vision for the world and outreach to LGBT people. I did not always understand it, but God called me into a process of faith, of suffering, rejection and shame with a goal of overcoming. Through the years I have felt called both to the LGBT people and to the church. It has been a very hard journey at times, but thanks be to God for victory, redemption and amazing "broomstick breakthroughs" that occurred.

A Story of Rejection and Redemption

Below is one story of a process I went through in interacting with my brothers and sisters in Christ. Let me begin by saying that I learned a lot through the years. God dealt with me in areas of immaturity and at certain times presumption. I am grateful for His kindness to me. I have also walked through rejection and misunderstanding from other Christians. Walking through this pain has been an important part of my quest for victory in Oz. It has changed me and prepared me to help others. I feel it has also resulted in significant change and healing in other believers. The story I share below is one example of beautiful redemption and restoration I have experienced with believers in many contexts.

Back in the late 80's I attended a convention. I was really excited about this particular meeting. They had a great worship team, dancers and vibrant preachers who operated in the spiritual gifts, especially in words of knowledge and prophecy. You could feel the atmosphere charged with the electric presence of God and the teachings were straight from heaven. It's hard to explain unless you've experienced it.

During the worship time a crowd of people who were full of incredible energy were dancing, singing and moving to the rhythms of the music. I went straight to the front because of my excitement and wanted to be in the middle of it. I loved experiencing God and His presence! After dancing a bit wildly with the rest I got pulled aside by one of the elders and told that I needed prayer to be set free from an "effeminate spirit." I was confused, hurt and also angered. I was upset that this correction was done in public view. I felt that all I was doing was pouring my heart out to God. I felt pressured because he was pushing to pray for me but I didn't feel any love in this approach or desire to understand me. I felt very judged. I left the conference and planned to never return.

At times like this I would sometimes relapse into some old behaviors because of my anger. I had a tendency whenever I was hurt unjustly, usually by authority figures, to revert to some kind of comfort, usually sexually. God helped me get back on my feet after stumbling again. God was healing my heart from that rejection.

When this summer conference came the next year the Lord told me to go back. I didn't want to. He told me that I had a key for the conference leader's future destiny. He didn't tell me what or why, but whatever was meant to happen I needed to show up in love in order to develop a relationship, whether they liked me or not. This time instead of a public correction, I was invited ahead of time by a different leader to feel free to dance in the back of the room instead of the front. I felt hurt and angry again...I had the same reaction as before and the Lord had to help me rise up again. It was difficult for me to handle rejection from what I considered to be family members, especially my Christian ones that I loved so much. Those you love the most can hurt you the most.

The third year came around. Oh boy. The Lord told me to go again and so I did. It wasn't easy but for the sake of what I sensed God had in store I did. This time, to my surprise, I was invited to put together a dance presentation with a small group of dancers. I was a bit leery because of the last two years. I didn't understand why I was invited to do this. I sought assurance asking the leader if the main host truly wanted me to do this and she said yes. So, I did it. During the presentation in front of about 200 people the entire dance team, including myself, were asked to stop and come to the back of the room. A leader said to the group, "someone here has pride!" I suddenly felt as though an arrow on fire hit my heart. I could sense that I was under the gun again. I asked if it was me? She strongly declared "YES!" Honestly, I was devastated. I was wounded. I felt rejected and judged with a sense of prejudice against me because of my background. I felt targeted by bullies. It was similar story I experienced many times my entire life from "family members" both natural and spiritual. I felt like a punching bag and I couldn't understand why this kept happening.

Dorothy showed a little courage when in the chamber of Oz. I felt a similar strength to speak. I invited the leader to lunch and told him how upset I was by the treatment I had received. I was furious. I didn't feel I deserved this kind of treatment and didn't want others to go through what I went through. At the time, the leader had stated publicly that he had a heart for gays. I believed him, but I felt his actions and those under his leadership conveyed the opposite. It was an honest conversation and was a good step, even though a difficult one.

I continued to believe God had a plan and had me engaged for some great purpose. Truly, there was a "broomstick breakthrough" ahead. Six months later the same person had a donors' luncheon for those who supported his ministry. Of course (I was not surprised) God spoke to me the fourth time about going to a ministry meeting. After the past three years of negative experience and anger, accompanied by my own hurt and sinful reactions, I had to really work out a deep level of forgiveness and release. I was having to go back with an open heart for a relationship that only God could create. I personally didn't see much light at the end of this tunnel. You can't make people like you, even if you're wearing the ruby slippers of God's favor.

At this luncheon there were about 50 leaders in attendance from the region. The key leader began to share that he had a heart for Kenya, Africa, and wanted to ship his books to help support Bible colleges and different ministries in that area.

Suddenly I was beginning to realize why God was having me go through this process and the pain of rejection. This man didn't know I had been going yearly to Kenya as a special guest speaker in the major convention Dome in downtown Nairobi, as well as other areas. I was a keynote speaker every year and was teaching workshops on prophetic worship, dance, arts and outreach. I had permission to invite anyone I wanted to be a speaker with me the next time I went. I then acted and invited this leader to join me the following year as a guest speaker and he accepted. He had no idea I had been going there. This was the key God revealed to me in a prophetic way about this minister's future. This was the "broom-stick breakthrough!"

The next year we arrived at the Dome in Nairobi. I introduced him to a friend who had a dream of starting Bible schools. This leader, that I initially had issues with, continued to go back to Kenya for 17 years and helped to establish Bible colleges from the east to the west coast of Africa! A few years later he brought in a well known international ministry based in California and part-nered with them in developing a multi-million dollar orphanage and discipleship training center. They took orphaned children off the streets whose parents had died from AIDS. The Vice President of Kenya called this a model center for all of Kenya.

This is a beautiful story of redemption. Despite turbulent begin-nings this leader and I are now dear friends and have become like close family. He wrote a book and dedicated a few pages to affirm-ing me and was very descriptive of how God used me in Africa.

Now he always tells me that I'm one of his favorites and invites me to speak at his conventions. He also speaks at my conferences. This friendship has been a great win. Patience with each other and forgiveness for offenses equals destiny for nations. Our story and journey together I think holds promise for believers everywhere and for healing with the body of Christ and those who may seem different, but who are truly fellow believers.

Paul the Apostle prayed that God would open the eyes of our hearts to see the riches of the glorious inheritance that is within the saints. The Wicked Witch of the West tried to cover the eyes of those that were to inherit a destiny and a blessing from those who were thought to be less than. God hides special treasures in people that are unseemly. These spiritual treasures can only be mined through humility and a true heart.

Dorothy had to prove herself by defeating the witch of rejection. Now her requests could be granted.

My journey has been one of finding my heart, courage and family. I was learning to do unto others as I would have them do unto me and to give rather than to receive. I had to get over being a victim and a scapegoat as I had been for so long. I was beginning to understand the unfathomable power of love and that forgiveness is one of the greatest keys to God's power.

Discovering the power of forgiveness and blessing, I am sharing a poem that my friend Grace taught me to live by. I have had to walk this poem out over and over with others throughout the years. It always works! It's so amazing how forgiveness and love conquers all pride and prejudice.

They drew a circle and shut me out
Heretic, Rebel, a thing to flout
But love and I had the wit to win
We drew a circle and brought them in.

Edward Markham

Chapter 20

The Witch's Castle

Let Him kiss me with the kisses of His mouth, for His
Love Is more delightful than wine.

Song of Songs 1:2

(Old Testament divine romance book)

Flying Monkeys and the Witch's Castle

Dorothy along with her heart, mind and courage are now in the dark forest. The Wicked Witch of the West is sending monkeys to capture her. These monkeys land on Dorothy's back lifting her off the ground taking her on wings to the witch's castle. There the witch locks Dorothy in captivity and turns over an hour glass, giving her only so much time to hand over the ruby slippers of destiny.

There have been times in my life when I struggled with "monkeys on my back." I'm using this metaphor to represent old former addictive thought patterns that want to make you captive again to sin. The scripture says "to lay aside every weight and the sin that so easily entangles, so that we may run the race" (Hebrews 12:1) and "win the prize of our high calling in Christ" (Philippians 3:14).

I was relapsing to the point that I almost lost hope. The hourglass was running out. One day as I was walking down the street parts of my body went numb. I thought I was having a stroke from the drugs. I just stood there detached, willing to die. I felt that I had let God down, as well as everyone I had loved. I didn't want to live anymore. Instead of having a stroke or a heart attack, I was actually overwhelmed by peace. God touched my heart and showed me He was there. There were many experiences I had during that two year struggle where God showed me He was there and that He loved me. I thought I had lost it all but my heavenly Father's love showed me that I hadn't.

Grace was keeping in touch with me during this time trying to encourage me. She shared with me that when she had gone to a prayer meeting, she stood up and declared like a lion "He is mine!" She claimed me in Christ and angels were released on that declaration to save me. God came through her prayers and the prayers of others that truly loved me. I heard that some Christian friends who truly loved and were thankful for me, had been woken up in the middle of the night to pray for me. I was never alone even though I felt very alone.

During this time I was excelling at my sales job where I was a trainer and manager. I was on the fast track to be promoted and would be moving to Melbourne, Australia, with full expenses paid, beginning a start-up business with my company. I was not doing well emotionally. I was in active addiction but no one at work seemed to know. Although this was an incredible opportunity, I knew that If I went it would have been the beginning of the end. I needed God to rescue me because I didn't know what to do. Grace heard a word from God that I was to come back to Spokane. There was such a sense of peace and relief that I knew it had to have been from God. As a result of God speaking to Grace, I was delivered from the witch's castle of captivity. I put myself into a treatment center in Spokane. Getting guidance from God as Grace did would be called "a word of wisdom," one of the spiritual gifts exercised in the church in Corinth, Greece. The word of wisdom is getting knowledge for a direction from

God. Without the gifts of the Spirit I couldn't have made it through the journey like I have. I need all of God in order to have Him have all of me.

Rainbow Flower Arises

I noticed something significant happening to me after I was released from the inpatient program. It was about a month later that I noticed something was missing inside of me. I wasn't sure what it was but it felt really good. It was as if a light bulb had gone off and I realized that a root of "anger" was missing from my soul. I began to feel peace and love bloom from within the center of my being. It was a new inner peace and love flowering into my consciousness nonstop and continues to this day. I remember what I wrote when in Las Vegas, God showed me a rainbow rise up and became as a flower in the sky. I now experienced that rainbow flower rising from the storm of my soul.

Dysfunctional Families Kill...Functional Families Heal

I realized that the reason the root of anger was dislodged out of my subconscious was because I was in an intense treatment center that was actually like a surrogate family! I never had any brothers growing up. This was all men who had much in common and were all there for the same reasons. There was no shame. We were all at the bottom.

I thank God for Sun Ray Court Treatment Center. It was truly a ray of sunshine that began to dawn in the deepest core of my beliefs and in my worth as a person. It also increased my faith that God is my Father. Because they role modeled support, healthy discipline, promotion, acceptance, dignity and respect as a family, I was able to experience a true family model.

Because of this, I had become free of needing family approval. I got a new perception that I was OK. It was like the blockage was gone. I would begin to bring acceptance and a feeling of family to others that I had always wanted for myself. People say they feel love, respect, dignity and healing when they are around me. I help to start groups wherever and whenever I can to help facilitate a feeling of true family. Jesus came not for a religion but for a family.

Many LGBT people have felt orphaned, even while in families, but God has healing for the heart. As I continue to persevere with resilience through my weaknesses and struggles in life, God continues to work all things out for my good. He completes every good work He begins in us, if we give Him the chance. I've learned that He's done everything for me already and walks with me through my own choices. I'm the only one who slows things down. But God never let's me go and He continues to kiss my heart, so that I won't give up on our relationship.

I have now found myself progressively becoming everything I have wanted and desired from others.

The following poem of St. Francis of Assisi expresses this trans-formation:

> *Lord, make me an instrument of your peace:*
> *where there is hatred, let me sow love;*
> *where there is injury, pardon;*
> *where there is doubt, faith;*
> *where there is despair, hope;*
> *where there is darkness, light;*
> *where there is sadness, joy.*
>
> *O divine Master, grant that I may not so much seek*
> *to be consoled as to console,*
> *to be understood as to understand,*
> *to be loved as to love.*
> *For it is in giving that we receive,*
> *it is in pardoning that we are pardoned,*
> *and it is in dying that we are born to eternal life.*
> *Amen.*

Transgender with Flying Monkeys on his Back

I was speaking at a charismatic Women's Aglow national con-ference about my "Over the Rainbow story." After the meeting I took a walk downtown and prayed for God to be able to share the love of Jesus to some Dorothy somewhere. Nearby at a bus stop, I found myself standing next to a transgender male. He didn't seem to have had a sex change, and was dressed up as a lady, but seemed a bit drugged out and His wig was sagging. We said hello and I shared with him what I was doing in Denver. I shared my story with him. He took great interest and asked me if he could receive Jesus into his life as well. I said, "Certainly you can!" He then asked me to run with him to catch his bus, so that I could tell him how to give his heart to Jesus. By the time we made it to his city bus, it was ready to depart. He told the bus driver to wait so that he could pray to give his heart to Jesus. We prayed right there while the bus waited. He ran so fast in his captivity that the monkeys on his back flew right off and into the streets. I hope they were run over!

Chapter 21

The Toto Exchange

You can have your old slippers, just give me back Toto!
-Dorothy

The Witch is petting Toto as she tells Dorothy what a nice little dog she has. She then tells her how kind it was to visit her in her loneliness. Dorothy asks the Witch what she's going to do with her dog and asks her to give Toto back. In response the Witch replies (in the movie) "All in good time my pretty, all in good time."[1] Dorothy pleads for the return of Toto, her heart of love. The Witch tries to work out a deal to exchange true love for the ruby slippers of power. Dorothy says to the Witch, "You can have your old slippers, but give me back Toto!" The Witch reaches for the God-slippers and the power zaps her! She remembers that the slippers would never come off unless Dorothy personally gave them up. That's right. As long as we stay in our faith, whether we're weak, struggling or in captivity, the ruby slippers of God's favor still stay upon our feet. I love this scripture that says,

Do not rejoice against me, o my enemy. Though I have fallen, I shall rise. Though I dwell in darkness, the Lord, He is my Light!
Micah 7:8

---

1 (LeRoy & Fleming, 1939).

LGBT Charismatic Pride Parade

The L.ove G.od B.e T.rue church in the New testament (the Grecian church) which consisted of former male temple prostitutes, homosexuals and effeminate men who had their own over-the-rainbow experiences, were very knowledgeable about God and excelled in the supernatural gifts of the Spirit. Because of that they had a tendency towards spiritual pride even though they came from a corrupt pagan culture. Because God so richly loves and forgives us, we are to freely use our spiritual gifts as expressions of that love for others. Paul the Apostle, their spiritual father of the faith, had to teach them that love was not boastful, rude or self seeking. He wanted them to be mighty in the spirit as true saints and to be mindful of God's gift of mercy while remaining humble.

When Dorothy chose love over power and was willing to give up the slippers she then became worthy of the ruby slippers' power. That was the defining moment when God's power in her life would reveal His love to those that Jesus died for...which was everyone.

The Witch Blocks Dorothy from her Family

The Witch leaves and begins to devise a scheme to get the ruby slippers. Dorothy is left weeping and she looks into the witch's crystal ball seeing her Auntie Em appear. She speaks to the image in the crystal ball telling of her plight, but to no avail. Auntie Em's face disappears and is replaced by the Witch who mocks her for trying to connect with her family.

There's something about satan not wanting us to connect with our families. That is the theme of this story. It's about God reconciling everyone to Him and to each other through Christ.

Here are some miracle stories of God using me to bring the love and power of Christ to estranged family members.

Family Members and a Christmas Miracle

While visiting my Grandma Nan in the hospital, I reconnected with my aunt and her daughter. They invited Grace and me to their house. My aunt, who I hadn't seen for years, had lung cancer and had a short time to live. I shared with them about my ministry in Russia, Israel, England and Africa. They were shocked. They thought I was a mess and just struggling in life according to the rumors and things they had heard. My aunt asked me if I would officiate her funeral when she passed away. I couldn't believe it and was so honored at her request. I then asked her if she'd like to have a spiritual touch from God and if I could pray for her. She agreed. Something amazing happened. My aunt expressed that she was feeling as though something was fluttering inside her chest. I took that to be like the "wings" of the Holy Spirit that was coming into her. She was actually opening her heart to Jesus and was receiving the dove.

She then said that she was able to breathe. My aunt then took out her oxygen tubes and was able to fully breathe for 2 hours! Her daughter, very close and dear to her, was watching her mom have some kind of miracle. I asked her if she would like to receive Jesus into her heart. I didn't stop there and also asked if she would like to receive her heavenly prayer language. She agreed to it all. As we were praying she fell out onto the floor under the presence of God speaking in heavenly tongues! After this encounter she shared that she had a series of visions about God's purpose for her future! They were both Mormons and believed in God but had never had a spiritual experience with Jesus and the Holy Spirit like this.

It was the day before Christmas and they were both filled with heavenly peace and my aunt was no longer afraid of dying. Suddenly there was a knock at the door. When we opened the door it was little girl who looked like an angel standing there all alone asking if she could sing us a song. We were more than willing to hear it. She began to sing the Christmas carol "Silent Night."

Silent night, Holy night. All is calm. All is bright. Round yon virgin, mother and child. Holy infant so tender and mild. Sleep in heavenly peace. Sleep in heavenly peace.

We were all taken aback by this little girl and her song on the day before Christmas. How could she have known that moments before both mother and daughter had received Jesus...the heavenly peace. It was truly a most holy night where all was now calm and all was now bright.

My aunt passed away soon after that glorious time. I was the officiant of her funeral. God's peace and love was tangibly felt at the funeral and people experienced it.

I moved away from Spokane and didn't have contact with my cousin for about year. As I was driving back into Spokane to visit family and friends the Lord prompted my heart to call my cousin to see how she was doing. The Lord spoke to me that she was still grieving over her mother's death and He wanted to give her a special gift if she would allow me to pray for her again. So I called her and shared the message. She agreed. When I placed my hand upon her head and began to pray, she gasped and looked shocked. I asked what was happening. She began to describe a vision she was seeing. Her mom and dad were in Paradise standing on the bank of a beautiful river along with other family members. God wanted to heal her of grief through that vision. That was the special gift He gave her. It was beautiful.

Dorothy, through God's love and power, was used to restore and bless her family members.

Chapter 22

Water on the Witch

As the hourglass is running out of sand, Dorothy calls out for her friends to hurry and save her. With an ax they chop through the door and come to her rescue. They have brought her little dog Toto with them, returning him to her. Dorothy receives back the heart she had lost in captivity although she had not lost her relationship with God. She is still wearing the ruby slippers.

There are times we struggle with ourselves and there are times we may fall into captivity. We may feel we have lost our heart, mind and even the will to continue on with our faith. We can even feel completely alone and wonder if God has given up on us. Yet, because we even care is a sign that we are still wearing our ruby slippers. As the Psalm of the Good Shepherd says, when our hearts fail, God is greater than our hearts and His mercy and goodness continues to follow us all the days of our life.

Dorothy's friends helped her to escape. She regained her heart to live and believed God's promises in her life, even though it appeared she failed in her journey. The mind of Christ comes back to her along with her heart of love and the reality of truth. God has come to her rescue because she is His child. She is under His divine favor and protection from all evil that has tried to trap, intimidate, and sow fear throughout her entire life, whether at home in Kansas, or on her spiritual journey over the rainbow.

Dorothy escapes with her mind renewed, with newfound courage and with a heart full of faith. Just as she and her friends are at the final door of escape they hear the cackling of the Witch as she blocks their escape with her guards surrounding them. She then instructs her guards to not hurt them right away, but rather to let them think about their circumstances for awhile.

I was held captive once again to my thinking and old behaviors which made it seem almost impossible to find my way of escape. I remember Michael Jackson in the *The Wiz*, playing the part of the Scarecrow. He sang, "Come on now, ease on down, ease on down the road." For me there was no easing down the road. When the Witch told the guards to let Dorothy think about her circumstances, it represented the fight for faith and identity and the internal battle that ensues with the struggle. Surrendering the ruby slippers would have been easing on down the road, but their power is so worth the fight.

I think for an LGBT person it can be very difficult. You wonder if it's all worth it? I had the impression when I went to the Emerald City that the rest of my life would be experiencing joy while laughing my days away in the Merry Ol' Land of Oz. I thought the Wizard had my best interests in mind. The pastors and teachers were preaching about the blessings in Christ and how awesome the power of God was to deliver us all from our sins. I heard that the Church was the family of God and how we are all to love one another and learn to walk in our spiritual gifts and ministries. Of course I also heard about the tribulations Christians go through to make it through their journey and into the full identities and destinies in Christ. I didn't want Christianity to be about struggling and spiritual warfare. I wanted it to be easy. It was a hard lesson to find that the Christian community wasn't always as loving and supportive as I had wanted them to be. I had had enough trauma at home in my natural Kansas family. I needed and wanted it to be easier. I needed help in learning how to ease on down the road. So there were times I had to re-think if I was able and willing to surrender more of my heart, mind and courage in this overcoming process. I always had to remember my vows at the Hollywood Gay Pride Parade where I had my first encounter with God. It was the vow that if He would save me, I would dedicate the rest of my life to Him and would never give up no matter how hard it might be. Whenever I would truly think about the price to pay to keep my inheritance of those powerful ruby slippers, I would remember that Jesus forgave me of all my sins and gave me the gift of eternal life and the honor of intimacy with God. I could never think of any reason to give up or ultimately go back to the way I used to be before my "over the rainbow" experience. God has given me so much more than I could ever have asked or imagined. I had to remember that the only reason the witch of fear, doubt and unbelief would attack me was for the purpose of subjugation. Satan hates us all and doesn't want us to inherit any of God's spiritual blessings. I've had to constantly fight to keep my inheritance that my heavenly Father gave me. My whole life has been about birthright, inheritance and the love God has always had for me as His chosen baby. He gave me beauty for ashes, joy for mourning and the garments of praise for the spirit of heaviness that I might be the display of His splendor and a minister of God.

Dorothy's Heart, Mind and Courage Work Together

The Witch takes hold of the hourglass and throws it at their feet. Broken, it releases a poisonous gas. The Scarecrow begins "to think" of a way to save Dorothy. He sees a wooden chandelier and grabbing the Tin Woodman's hand, swings the axe at the ropes, causing the chandelier to crash on the Witch's guards. The Witch screams at the guards to seize them as they begin to chase them. The Scarecrow begins leading the way with the mind of Christ, helping Dorothy, her heart and the truth escape the deception that has been holding them captive.

As they escape the main part of the castle they become surrounded on all sides. The Witch shows up again raising her broomstick to a burning lamp setting it on fire. She begins to taunt the Scarecrow and says, "How about a little fire, Scarecrow?"

The Witch was always trying to set the Scarecrow on fire. She is always trying to ruin our thinking and keep us from God's truth and wisdom. She wants us to stay distracted and to stay conformed to our old thought life and patterns of who we are outside of Christ. She knows when we begin to understand our true identity in Christ, as saints and overcomers, she will be defeated. She doesn't want LGBT to become L.overs of G.od B.eing T.rue.

The Scarecrow catches fire and Dorothy grabs a bucket of water that she sees close by. As she throws the water on the Scarecrow to put out the flames, water sprays the Witch.

The Bible speaks of water as the word of God. The water of the word puts out the fires of hell. Having meditated on the Word of God, it gave me something to work with. Fighting the good fight of faith comes from knowing the words of God and having them stored in our heart. King David said in the book of Psalms that he could avoid sin more if he stored the word of God in his heart.

When the water hits the Witch, she screams at Dorothy. She cries out that she's melting as she sinks in a hellish mist, this time going down into the earth and not the mist. She outwardly exclaimed her confusion, that such a good little girl could destroy my beautiful wickedness?[1] Dorothy had a good heart, like my Grandmother used to say about me, and in the end, through Christ, it destroyed beautiful wickedness!

How amazing it seems to me that I could destroy the beautiful wickedness of the witch that held me captive so many times throughout my life. I had often felt so much like a victim but it was truly the ruby slippers which God gave me that made me who I am as a L.over of G.od B.eing T.rue!

---

1 (LeRoy & Fleming, 1939).

God has given me everything for life. He has given me His overcoming Holy Spirit that sets me free from all the power of carnal orientations and gives me new spiritual orientations, making me heavenly instead of earthly. I'm becoming more and more heavenly minded now that I'm actually becoming "earthly good!"

Thy Kingdom Come on Earth as it is in Heaven

When I prayed the Lord's Prayer at that parade, I said "Thy kingdom come, Thy will be done, on earth as it is in heaven." I didn't realize heaven was about to be imparted to me after a rainbow ride into Oz. Nor did I realize that when I became born of the Spirit, that I was now a child of a new birth, with a new orientation and a new nature. I became a heavenly minded man and would learn how to release the Spirit of the kingdom through my words. Jesus said we would have the power to love from God's love, heal the sick, cast out evil spirits, speak in new tongues and cleanse lepers. Heaven will heal those who are HIV Positive and will bring forth JC Positive (Jesus Christ Positive)!

I declare over LGBT that the grace of heaven is coming to you, either for the first time or again and more powerful than ever before. Today as you read this the word of God is releasing you from your captivity. You are forgiven. You are loved with an everlasting love and every demonic spirit released to bind you from God's peace, that is found in Jesus, must go now! In Jesus' mighty name be free from the fire of hell. The fire which has tried to steal from you, kill you, destroy you and rob you of your birthright in Christ along with every spiritual and natural blessing God has for you! You have a purpose. You have a hope and a future. Wake up sleeper. Arise from the dead and Christ will shine on you!

Chapter 23
The Witch's Broom

Dorothy, now having possession of the Witch's broom returns to the Emerald City to present it to the Wizard. As she approaches the large, looming face, she tells the Wizard that they have done what he had asked. She brought him the broomstick of the Wicked Witch of the West and told him they had melted her.

The Wizard, seeing Dorothy with the Witch's broom, condescendingly remarks about how resourceful she is, then tells her to go away.

Even though Dorothy persevered through threats, fireballs, fears, and her own weaknesses, she is still not validated by the Wizard.

She gave her all in her new life despite many hard struggles. She listened intently to the sermons and teachings of the wizards and much to their surprise was accomplishing what they were preaching. She fought lions and tigers and bears...oh my! She rose from the poppies and came out of captivity. She proved her faith in God.

Dorothy thought they would finally celebrate her when she accomplished such amazing feats only to be told that she should go away. One would think the Wizard would have appointed her to his counsel because of her insights from battle experiences.

Although the Wizard told Dorothy to come back tomorrow... when would tomorrow be? Would there ever be a tomorrow?

Dorothy was getting angry at this point and told him to stop blowing her off. She had the ruby slippers and put all the wizard's sermons and teachings into practice. She put the words of God into practice. She fought the witches, healed the sick, and preached the gospel. She led many to Christ and spearheaded inner city movements of God's love and power to the broken. She went by faith and mobilized teams in different nations. Dorothy's ministry was accompanied by signs, wonders and miracles. She got up when she fell down and confessed her sins. She continued to go forward when she was tempted to give up and stop trying. She was resilient. She bore the stigma of HIV-AIDS before her Christian family and talked honestly on television and radio about her humanity and God's divinity. She led musical parades in the streets of nations and was even transported supernaturally across town one night!

Supernatural Transportation

Jesus got into the boat and immediately they were on the other side.
John 6:21

One night I was driving downtown from a town nearby Spokane. I could see the city lights getting closer in front of me while I was driving westward. I had been driving quite a distance. While I was driving under some trees with branches and leaves covering the street, I suddenly found myself facing the opposite direction and near to where I had originally come from. I was really freaked out and thought to pinch myself, wondering what had just happened. It was a bit surreal. I knew that I was near Spokane, but suddenly ended up in what we call the Valley. I was in a place called Green Acres. There was a man named Royal who was a well known Christian prophet who lived there. His house was a block away from where I ended up. It was near midnight and I instinctively knew to go to his house and knock on the door. I felt awkward doing this because of it being so late and the fact that I didn't know the man very well although I felt quite sure this supernatural transportation brought me to his place for a reason. I remember reading about Christians and Old Testament prophets being taken from one place to another in different supernatural ways. I always wanted to experience that. The Bible says we can experience many things that are recorded if we can just believe it. This phenomena which happened to me took me by surprise. When I knocked at the door a young man in his 20's answered the door. It turned out that he was sitting there alone watching TV. He was in a deep depression for some reason. I told him how I go there which caused him to believe that God was giving him a special sign of His love. He must have been crying out to God to help him and then Angel showed up! We prayed together and he instantly came out of his depression and had a new hope.

86'd from an Orphanage

I had been invited by a friend from church to come and minister to orphans at a Christian orphanage in the woods in Central Oregon.

I was excited for such an opportunity, so I went. I assumed this was sanctioned by the directors or else I wouldn't have been invited.

When I arrived, there were about 40 little ones ranging from ages 8-14. House parents were with them and my friend was there. I gave a little message about forgiveness because these children had been abused in many ways–physically, emotionally and sexually. I wondered how a message of forgiveness would take with these little ones. How could you suggest to children to release forgiveness for things like that? Well you can, in the sense that forgiving others doesn't get them off the hook, it just gets you off their hook. Through forgiveness, you are no longer under the power of bitterness that can destroy the rest of your life.

Through the power and grace of the Spirit of God, He can supernaturally grace the heart with divine love and peace that will fill the hole created by the terrible wounds. God did that for me over time, He can do it for anyone. These orphans needed to not feel like orphans anymore. They needed a touch from their heavenly Father that would cause them to feel special and to believe that they were also God's chosen babies.

After my message, they all lined up for prayer. It blew my mind to hear them saying things like, "I want to forgive my dad" or "I want to forgive my mom." It brought tears to my eyes. One by one, as I laid my hand upon each little dear head, similar to feathers floating to the ground, these children floated down to the floor under the beautiful healing power of God. All of them were in tranquility under the influence of the Spirit of God's power and love. You could see their faces changing expressions as though God were flowing through their memories and healing them. It was like spiritual surgery. After about 20 minutes, they began to regain consciousness from their spiritual sleep states and would go to their friends and hold their heads in their laps until they came back to their normal states. Children started coming to me and sharing things such as: "Jesus just told me that I'm going to be a missionary in my future," or "God gave me a Bible scripture." They would then share the scriptures with me. Their heavenly Father was giving them identity and destiny words to give them a hope and a future! It was the most spiritual and beautiful thing I'd ever seen. I was invited to stay in the community for a few more days to hang out with them all if I wanted to. I did, and couldn't wait to see and hear more stories and the results of the orphans' divine encounters.

As most of them were laying peacefully on the floor under the divine presence of God, the Director suddenly came in. He hadn't been there, but I didn't think it mattered. The lady who invited me and all the house parents were there approving of this amazing ministry. They were blown away by what God was doing for these broken children they loved so much.

When the director walked in the door of this lodge, he couldn't believe what he saw. He didn't know what to make of it. He quickly walked out and called my pastor. He obviously knew I was coming and knew my pastor, but didn't expect God to show up. He must have thought that I'd give a little message. As for me, I usually expect God to show up. To me, messages aren't enough. He called my pastor to find out who this guy was that caused these orphans under his ministry to be all over the floor under the power of God. He wasn't pleased at all!

My pastor informed him of my past gay life and probably my HIV status. I was never told. This man immediately came back into the room, asking me to come outside. He then 86'd me from the orphanage! My heart was broken.

I went home where I was living with my birth mother which I share in another chapter. I told her what happened. I could feel a depression coming over me from the rejection after such a heavenly experience. The spirit of religion, metaphorically the Witch of the East, had once again tried to destroy my heart, mind and courage.

My mom understood how I felt and had an idea to help me get out of the depression. She invited me to a Women's Aglow luncheon where there was a wonderful woman named Evelyn speaking from Pennsylvania. My mom sensed that she had a gay son who passed away from AIDS complications. The woman, who was the speaker, wasn't really saying it to the group but my mom just read between the lines.

I decided to go with her and met this lady. I talked with her after her message and asked her if I could ask a personal question. She agreed. I then asked her if her son had passed away from AIDS. She nodded yes and said he was her only son. His name was Kurt.

She then relayed that he had a heaven encounter from God a couple weeks before he died. He resisted God his whole life and mocked Jesus with many of his LGBT friends for many years which broke her heart. She had been a believer and raised him with his salvation and his destiny in her heart. A lady named Joy Dawson, a director of Youth With a Mission, (YWAM), was her dear friend. She flew to Hollywood to begin praying for his salvation before he passed away. She began to fast and pray with all her heart. She told God she wasn't going to quit appealing to heaven until he had an encounter with God. And so he did!

Kurt saw a black book coming out of heaven from God's hands. God spoke audibly to him and told him that it was his life. Many pages were black, not cleansed by the blood of Christ. God wanted Kurt to confess his sin of independence from God and to turn to Jesus as Savior and Lord. Because of that vision from heaven, he did that. For the next two weeks he saw heaven open before him in 4D vision. Movie stars and others who would visit him were all hearing about what heaven was like, and who Jesus was as he was experiencing Him in real time! He had become blind because of the effects of his condition. He couldn't even see his mom or dad when they came to visit him. But one day, for a brief moment, God opened Kurt's eyes to see his parents there with him with a bouquet of flowers they had brought. Kurt's supernatural vision of heaven before him was so real and alive to him, that he begged his parents to help him get there. He said that he saw himself dancing on streets of gold and that he could literally feel the breeze of heaven blowing through his hair! His story is written about in a book that Joy Dawson wrote, called, *Intercession-Thrilling and Fulfilling.*

I told Evelyn that I would like to be her spiritual son since Kurt was in heaven and told her my story. She gave me a warm hug and said yes. We've been very close friends and have minis-tered together across the country. Kurt had a revelation that he shared with his mom. He said, "Mom, God revealed to me that I don't have to have any attractions towards females. He said that I could just have peace." He used to think that in order to give his life to God he had to have heterosexual attractions towards females and it was unimaginable for him. So, for him, he didn't come to Christ. He didn't realize that he could just have peace with God and not have to worry about it or try to prove to others that he wasn't gay. Dorothy was an enigma. Before God, she was celebrated. Before the wizards, not so much.

This was an amazing divine appointment I had after I was 86'd from the orphanage! I got the religious witch's broom of rejection!

I will prepare a table in the presence of your enemies.
Psalm 23:5

Chapter 24

Toto Exposes the Wizard

Pay no attention to the man behind the curtain.

From the movie, *The Wizard of Oz*[1]

Dorothy tells the Wizard if he really was great and powerful, he should keep his promises. He asks her loudly and forcefully if she "presumes to criticize the Oz?"[2] and calls them ungrateful creatures who should consider themselves lucky he was even giving them an audience.

As he continues to project his authoritative voice on to Dorothy, Toto, her heart of truth, senses something behind the curtain and trots over, pulling open the curtain. There an elderly man is speaking into a microphone. He's also working a control board which seem to be connected to the smoke and fire that's projecting the image. Dorothy sees Toto exposing this Wizard.

Dorothy had to learn the hard way that men or women of God were only human. At first she believed most everything they said. After all, they had the Holy Spirit and were mature in the things of God. They had the wisdom and the keys to the kingdom. Dorothy was told by these elders that she could also become a leader by following their guidance. They preached about spiritual authority and were to be respected and feared because of their position.

---

1 (LeRoy & Fleming, 1939).

2 (LeRoy & Fleming, 1939).

Wizards Misrepresenting the Heavenly Father

One elder, that I was living with told me that he was in the "office" of a father and made me take all of the rocks out of his rock garden to prove myself. I asked him if he could just be a father. He got very angry at me and invited me to leave his home. I did.

Another spiritual father, a "wonderful Wizard of Oz," who had an international ministry invited me to live with him as a spiritual son. I thought he might be a mentoring father that I had always dreamed of. He was a well known, spiritually developed prophet and said he had many encounters with Jesus appearing to him. People knew him for this and for his teachings. I could sense he had some very real experiences but it was eye-opening to see the real man behind the ministry.

When I moved in, he immediately ordered me to start working around the house and yard. I was in my 20's and wanting to be trained by such a spiritual father as this. He had me up at 6:00 a.m. and working for him until 11:00 p.m. I cleaned his house, worked in his wood shop, and in the garden, operated the tractor, edited his teaching tapes, ran his printing press and prayed for him over and over again when he'd nearly have heart attacks from being so high energy. This was his way to train me. If whatever he had me was using broke, he recorded it as future debt against me. I seemed to always be indebted to him and his ministry. He was wanting me to work for him for the rest of my life until I paid off all my debts to him. From his standpoint I would never work it off. It was a bit like the slave word. All in the name of discipleship. He would then compare my work ethic and energy level with his sons in the marines putting me to shame for being a loser because I wouldn't produce more for him than I already was. He got a little generous and gave me a $50 check once a month. Behind the pulpit he would talk about the great power and authority he had from God and how people would die if they betrayed him. At times he would affirm me publicly but I felt it was to manipulate that vulnerable place in my heart so he could get more out of me. I got so exasperated by what I began to believe was spiritual abuse that I literally cried out to God for seven things that were very important for me to change in my situation. I didn't know how long I could take it. I was afraid to leave because of the thought that maybe I needed this strict discipleship training. My Toto heart was picking up on the fact this man had his own agenda and my Toto pulled back the curtain.

A couple of weeks later after these prayers, a musical prophet came to this man's church. As he was singing he said there was someone in this church that asked God for seven things. He then said, "Whoever you are, God now has answers for each request." He began to speak out all seven of my requests as he was playing his guitar. I was blown away. God truly knew what was going on in my heart and was answering my prayers. I then realized for sure that something wasn't right. God was working some things out in my heart and life through this painful experience with someone who called himself my spiritual father. I went to my former pastor, Pastor Jim, who has always continued to be there for me whether I was going to his church or not. I asked him about possibly leaving, but my heart wasn't sure about what was really going on. He counseled me that when I couldn't stand another day then I should leave. I left that very same day. There were parts of this man behind the curtain that did have a gentleness about him. I really loved and liked him. I saw God in him and he mightily inspired my life to go deeper into God's presence. There was a part of him that really wanted to invest in my calling but he ended up using me for his own self-interest. A year later I ran into him at a conference and we talked. I thanked him for all he gave me and told him that I was very grateful for everything and our friendship was restored. I also told him the truth about feeling used and mistreated. I don't think there were many people who stood up to him because he was a "great and powerful Oz." This Dorothy did!

I soon left Spokane for Tacoma where I met Pastor Robert at a Church of God in Christ denomination. He believed that I was called into the ministry and had me preach in his church many times. This helped to restore my self worth. I began to go forward into my calling and I was soon launched into international ministry.

I have come to realize that just because people say they have encounters with Jesus doesn't necessarily mean they have their lives together. Jesus came to the apostle Paul when he was at his worst in order to show him how great His love and mercy was for him. He needed a vision of Jesus to get his life right with God. As a result Paul became one of the greatest heralds of the mercy and kindness of God. He reached out to the LGBT community in Corinth, Greece. His love and message was so filled with grace that the LGBT community came to his church and grew in great understanding of God. Jesus said that His true sheep wouldn't follow the voice of a stranger, but they would hear His voice and come to Him. Religion based in fear, guilt and shame that comes through the wizards is the voice of the stranger. Mercy, grace, kindness and patience, along with true fatherly discipline based in love comes from the True Shepherd Jesus. He leads us beside still waters, restores our souls, and yes, He does have a rod and staff of discipline and training, not to beat the gay out of the sheep, but to comfort and guide them. (Psalm 23)

Mean Wizards

Prophecy from Ezekiel 34: 1-6

> *God's message came to me: "Son of man, prophesy against the shepherd-leaders of My people. Yes, prophesy! Tell those shepherds, 'God, the Master, says: Doom to you shepherds of Israel, feeding your own mouths! Aren't shepherds supposed to feed sheep? You drink the milk, you make clothes from the wool, you roast the lambs, but you don't feed the sheep.*

*You don't build up the weak ones, don't heal the sick,
don't doctor the injured, don't go after the strays, don't
look for the lost. You bully and badger them. And now
they're scattered every which way because there was no
shepherd -scattered and easy pickings for wolves and
coyotes. Scattered -My sheep! exposed and vulnerable
and no one out looking for them!'''*
(The Message Bible)

Prophetic Word from Angel

Today, God is sending out his true shepherds to seek and find
the lost sheep that have been treated with meanness and abuse
in God's church. The cries of the broken have arisen to God's nose
and justice is on the way. A new movement of the Father, the
Son and the Holy Spirit is arising now to heal broken hearts, open
the eyes of the blind, set the captives free and to release from
inner prisons of shame and fear. LGBT is on the heart of God and
His hand of salvation is reaching out in great love and power to
find you and to bind your wounds and give you new beginnings.
He is working on spiritual shepherds' hearts to change and repent
of their harshness. If they don't, they will be dealt with by God
and it won't be fun for them.

God has true fathers, pastors and saints who are ready to
embrace you in a new gracious way. Your good shepherd Jesus,
represented by Glinda, will guide you to green pastures, being
people that will be a safe place for you, whether it's just one, two
or a group that will help heal, nurture and disciple you to become
all that God called you to be... "a L.over of G.od B.eing T.rue!"

Chapter 25

Dorothy's Rewards

I will restore the hearts of the fathers to the sons
and the hearts of the sons to the fathers.

Malachi 4:6

After the Wizard put Dorothy and her friends through many hoops, he couldn't deny they not only talked the talk, they also walked the walk. He finally opens his heart to her and treats her like a friend, turning his father's heart toward her. He bestows upon her heart wisdom and courage and his seal of approval and now attempts to help Dorothy get home...where the heart is.

The Wizard and Academic Theology

Academic Theology is the study of God through understanding scripture through study.

To the Scarecrow, the Wizard tells him of universities and schools of great learning. He shares with him that all he needs is a diploma. He then gives him a PhD degree of Thinkology. The Scarecrow asks the Wizard how he can ever thank him for this validation and ordination. The Wizard tells him that he can't.

All the Wizard has for the Scarecrow is an academic diploma. He is part of the clergy system based on intellectual attainment rather than experiential knowledge of God.

Credentials from God

I was visiting a church where a guest speaker functioning with the spiritual gifts of knowledge singled me out of the small congregation. This church leadership had titles such as Doctor, Bishop and Reverend, because you had to have professional titles in this particular denomination to be established as a credible minister. I didn't have any of these credentials but what I did have was a relationship with God and I was doing what Jesus taught believers to do through the power of my ruby slippers. The prophet in the congregation asked me to stand up and then said, "Many of you went to schools, got diplomas and certificates for ordained ministry but not this man. He has been trained by God, Himself and is called to America."

The Wizard now gives the cowardly lion a medal of honor and tells him that he is now a member of the Legion of Courage. The Wizard kisses him on both cheeks as the lion is in rapturous validation.

Dorothy and Experience Theology

Experience Theology is the art and science of knowing God experientially.

For some reason I had always desired and felt a need to become friends with spiritual fathers. It wasn't always just to receive something from them, but to also give something valuable in return that would aid their understanding and experience as well. I would find a spiritual father here and there in my younger years, but as I matured in Christ, I desired to be invited into their inner circles where they gathered as friends sharing theology. I was doing the works of Christ outside the four walls of the church much of the time because that was where the opportunities seemed to be. Jesus was ministering out in the world much more than in the synagogues. He was out among the people teaching them and demonstrating the power of the kingdom of God. I felt I needed spiritual fathers in order for me to fully mature. I wanted them to recognize the calling upon my life and the passion I had to go all the way for Christ. I wasn't a church pew warmer. I became a fire-brand and thought I was worth the investment with these fathers of the faith. What I could bring to the table is what I'm calling "experience theology." I believe academic theology is imbalanced if not mixed with experiential theology. When Jesus went through the villages He demonstrated experiential miracles first, and then He taught theology.

I learned to work with the Holy Spirit in the marketplace, on the streets and even in the church. We were taught to do this according to the example of Jesus and His disciples. While doing this I discovered much of the depth, width and breadth of God's love. Even though I gained much experience, I still felt uninvited into the inner circles. Nonetheless, I feel determined and con-tinue to move forward. I'm now becoming more of a spiritual teacher of God's ways, having gained much understanding of how He works in many ways through a close relationship with Him as well as studying His word.

A Broken Heart Clock and a Relational Testimony

In the movie, the Wizard gives the Tin Woodman a red heart clock on a chain.[1] It's only a token of love but the deeper love truly comes from the heavenly Father. The Wizard was trying to love the best he could. Before, he could only tolerate them but was now trying to empower them.

The heavenly Father, as you will read on, gave me something from his heart that really brought healing, love and life to me.

God's Heart Gives Angel His Birth Mother

I was visiting a friend of mine who lived in Spokane. She was an elderly lady who loved Jesus with all her heart and was a dear friend. She moved into my Grandma Nan's old house where I had

---

1 (LeRoy & Fleming, 1939).

spent so much time as a child. As I was sitting in her living room I had an encounter with God. We weren't praying, we were just visiting. As I am writing this, it just dawned on me that I was sitting on her couch in the exact same location where I would sit on my Grandma Nan's couch as a child, feeling her comfort when I was hurting. A downpour of spiritual liquid love, which felt like warm oil, flowed down from my head through my entire being. In that moment I was having a strong impression to search of my birth mother, whom I never knew. My adoptive mother always told me they would support me in finding her after I turned 18. They claimed to even possibly know her name. I shared this experience with another close friend of mine who was excited about this endeavor. We went to a local adoption agency and filled out all the paperwork.

In a very short time they called me and told me they had found her. They discovered she lived in Albany, Oregon but couldn't open my records because they were sealed. The search continued and my birth mother was finally found through her father's obituary. The adoption agency had me write a one page letter to her which they would forward. I wrote a letter thanking her for giving me up for adoption and told her she did the right thing and that I was doing well. I shared a little bit about my faith in Jesus and told her that I would love to meet her, if that is what she wanted. I didn't want her to feel obligated or responsible for me in any way, but it would be a great blessing to be friends. The agency gave her my phone number and she called. It was very exciting to be talking to my birth mother for the first time. She told me when she read my letter she shook and cried all day. Her present husband was not my birth father. She stated my father had been a professional actor in Hollywood and they had only known each other for a very brief time. I didn't recognize his name. I thought that was very interesting because I had gone to Hollywood in 1983 to pursue an acting career. She didn't know where he was but gave me a clue that would help me find him if I so desired. I have never had a strong desire to find him.

My birth mother shared that we had Jesus in common and she had received Him a year after I had. She was also active in a Christian organization called "Women's Aglow." That was amazing to me. Women's Aglow is a charismatic Christian organization that has luncheons with people that practice ministering in the spiritual gifts written about in Bible to other women.

A Gay Friend, Salvation and Healing of AIDS

My birth mother and I decided we wanted to meet face to face. She drove all the way from Albany to Spokane to meet me. I was living on a beautiful piece of land called Living Springs Ranch in a cabin called the Galilee. A famous book was written in this cabin called *Nine O'clock in the Morning*. It was written by a world renown Episcopal Priest named Dennis Bennett. This book was about how the Holy Spirit swept the world and every denomination, including the Catholics, with the charismatic gifts of the Holy Spirit, including the gifts of speaking in tongues and prophecy. This famous cabin became the first place my birth mother and I would spend two weeks together sharing our lives. I took my mom to a picturesque pond at the ranch on a beautiful spring day. Taking my guitar we sang songs about Jesus, cried and just held each other. She told me her father had wanted her to have an abortion. She was 24 when she gave birth to me and I found her when I was 24. We compared pictures of us at the same age and almost looked like twins. My birthmother came to Spokane that year and spent time with my adoptive mother and father. We were all together.

I shared with my birth mother about my life, the homosexuality and my HIV status. She wasn't thrilled to hear about it but was very loving and kind. She felt my life may have been better had she not given me up for adoption but when she told me what her life was like, I'm not so sure. I think God chose who I would be raised by because he had a purpose for my life. The beautiful thing about all this is that I am connected to these two wonderful families. I have a good relationship with both of my mothers.

Everything is forgiven between all of us and our unity is now in Jesus. Though none of us are perfect and we're all on our own journeys, there's so much goodness that God has in us, for us and through us to others. I am just so thankful for the wonderful wisdom of God in putting all of this together.

In the two weeks my birth mother and I were at the ranch, I was able to take her downtown to the streets and introduce her to people I knew. We ran into a friend who was active in gay prostitution. I introduced them. They immediately liked each other and we both decided to invite him to our cabin to have dinner and stay overnight. He was happy to accept. Being weak and frail, I had to hold his arm while walking him from the car into the cabin. We just hung out and he shared that he had full blown AIDS and was given a death sentence from the doctor and had only a few months to live. He told us that he wanted to receive Jesus into his heart. So we prayed with him and he gave his heart to the Lord. The next morning he and I were sitting together and I asked him if I could pray with him to receive the gift of the Holy Spirit and to pray for his healing. It states in Psalm 103 that God forgives every sin and heals diseases. The Bible also says that by the stripes Jesus received in our place, we can at times receive healing. I called my mom into the living room to be a part of this prayer. She came and as I laid my hand upon his head to receive the gift of the Spirit he fell out on the floor under the power of God. He was vibrating on the floor as his new heavenly language was flowing out of his mouth. When this experience was over he stood up and his face was bright and shining. He told us that he felt so different and a new energy had come into his body. He felt that he could run laps around our cabin and knew Jesus had come into his heart through the indwelling of the Holy Spirit. He also shared that the pain from the AIDS was leaving his body and wondered if he had received a divine healing. Within a week he called me and said the sores from his skin had disappeared and the doctors had given him a new report. He said that the effects of AIDS was totally gone. My mom and I recorded this story in the Galilee cabin guest book which is still on record to this day. This experience happened in 1988. He didn't die of AIDS and moved to Seattle. I didn't see him for the next eight years. Later, when I ran into him, he told me that his life was going well and he was still healthy.

Adoption God-cidences!

Moving to Oregon, I lived with my birth mother and her husband for two years. She had me speak at one of her Women's Aglow luncheons. None of her friends knew she had given up a child for adoption and it was quite a story for them to hear. We then joined a church together in Corvallis, Oregon. She became the secretary and I became a worship leader. We began to pray for people who had given children up for adoption and also those who had been adopted. Miraculously quite a few suddenly began to find their family members. One lady who came through this church and taught healing from sexual abuse had given up her baby at birth because she had been raped by her father. Two weeks after my birth mother and I prayed for her to find her daughter, she God-cidentally found her! It was an amazing story and totally unexpected. She talked to her daughter for the first time in her life and discovered that she had been adopted by a Christian pastor and his wife. They were reunited.

Jews, Mennonites, Circuit Preachers and Native Americans

My birth mother took me to her 100th year family reunion. I was now beginning to discover my genealogy. I found out many of my relatives were religious. One side of my family were German Jews according to my cousin. I was told they migrated from Germany to Poland and then on to Russia. Because of the persecution under the Czar they became Mennonites. They then migrated to the United States and started a prune orchard in The Dalles, Oregon. My name was placed on the family tree so that everyone could see. There was a part of me that always seemed to be missing and now I had finally found my roots. On my birth mother's father's side there were Methodist circuit preachers. Some of them had worked with the Cherokee Indians during their persecution on the Trail of Tears. I visited that location a year ago while visiting Hot Springs, Arkansas. My heart broke for the Native Americans and how they were treated. I was so thankful I came from a line that had compassion for them.

Jesus Rescues a Gay Native American

I'm reminded of a panhandling, gay Native American in Seattle that I met on Broadway Avenue. Grace and I invited him over for a beautiful dinner with expensive silverware and china. We wanted him to feel special and respected. He gave his heart to Jesus as a result and had an amazing encounter with God when visiting our L.ove G.od B.e T.rue home church in Capitol Hill. As he was lying peacefully on the floor he had a vision. In this vision from God he saw warriors standing in two rows by a river holding giant spears. He said there was a baby drowning in the water and none of the warriors noticed. Then he shared that in his vision Jesus walked out of nowhere toward the soldiers. They all parted as Jesus made His way to the river to rescue the drowning baby.

Grace and I understood the interpretation. This man was the drowning baby in the river of the world. The soldiers were some Christians who didn't notice. Jesus coming to his rescue represented someone inviting him over for dinner, treating him with dignity and respect, helping him to experience God's power and love on a very personal basis. His life was never the same and he got much healing in his heart and became one of our dearest friends. We've lost touch with him over the years but we hope to see him again.

The Fatherly Wizard Now Chooses To Take Dorothy Home

Dorothy's friends are so excited because of the rewards they received from the Wizard and are sharing them with her. She does her best to express her joy for her friends. The Scarecrow suddenly notices that Dorothy didn't get anything and is feeling left out. He asks the Wizard what he's going to do for Dorothy. Dorothy, with watery eyes comments that she doesn't believe that there's anything in the Wizard's bag for her.

The Wizard tells her that she has forced him into a cataclysmic decision. The only way for Dorothy to get back to Kansas is for him to take her back himself. Rather than making appointments and preaching to her, he is now willing to be a fatherly friend for the common goal. Dorothy needed a father to get back home.

Chapter 26

Toto's Freedom

Perfect love casts out all fear.
1 John 4:8 (NIV)

Toto's Transformation from Fear to Love

As I am writing this, something amazing dawned on me. In the beginning of the movie, Dorothy's neighbor, the mean Miss Gulch, was trying to destroy Toto. Toto escaped from her in great fear, running back home to find Dorothy. Toto represents Dorothy's inner heart of truth and integrity. Through fear, dark forces were working to disintegrate Dorothy as a child of God. Dorothy's Uncle Henry represented the only father figure she had ever known. To Dorothy, Auntie Em and Uncle Henry didn't understand the importance of her heart by making her give Toto away to Miss Gulch to be destroyed.

The story ends with Toto jumping out of a basket. This time it's not the basket of a witch, but a loving spiritual father...the wonderful Wizard of Oz. Toto sees an attractive female dog somewhere in the crowd. It was love at first sight and Toto ran after it.

Dorothy's Toto heart of truth and integrity was almost destroyed by fear in the beginning, but by the end of the journey, Toto ran toward love. Dorothy's life had disintegrated but had been integrated at the end. As the scriptures say, "perfect love drives out all fear." This transformational story is about love conquering all fear...an unhealthy fear of God, man, failure and dark forces. God sent Jesus into the world to deliver it from the power of fear, sin and death. I have received a powerful revelation of God's love which has brought me new life.

At a conference years ago, another speaker singled me out and said "A time is coming in your future when you, similar to the caterpillar, will come out of a cocoon. But you will not come out as a butterfly, you will come out as an eagle."

Eagles are not victims to fear and intimidation. They thrive on storms and they eat snakes. Snakes speak of shame but Jesus replaces all shame with dignity.

Dorothy found the Father's love and was finally home at last. Her heart was at rest, her mind was enlightened with the truth and courage came back to stand against lies.

> *There is no fear in love, but perfect love drives out fear,*
> *because fear involves punishment. The one who fears*
> *has not been perfected in love.*
> *We love because He first loved us.*
> *John 4:18-19*

I had a Dream

I once had a dream where I was up in the air and saw a mystical stone with some kind of inscription on it. As I zoomed down toward the stone, the inscription changed into English so I could read it. It said, "Get understanding and all shall be filled." I saw a book appear in the air. It was called, *The Pleasures of Loving God*, written by Mike Bickle. Next, I saw myself around my spiritual age of 33 and I was resting, standing up but leaning in a sacred repose in my heavenly Father's arms of love.

I realized that as I would find the pleasure of loving God, that I would understand how to enter the sacred repose in my Father's arms. All my troubles would melt like lemon drops and I would no longer be or feel like an orphan. I would be in the center of God's loving heart.

Get this book, *The Pleasures of Loving God*, and learn how to find ultimate pleasure in the arms of God, who will never leave or forsake you. He will never betray you or abuse you. People do, even in God's name, but God never does. He doesn't hate you. He not only loves you, He actually likes you! He wants you to really get to know Him, so that you can love and like Him too!

This song just came to my mind from the musical, *The King and I*. I believe that King Jesus is singing this song to whoever is reading this. He wants to know you more and for you to know Him more. He's calling you to an intimate relationship. He wants to be your Lover! You don't have to be alone.

Getting to know you, Getting to know all about You.
Getting to like you, getting to hope that you like me
Haven't you noticed? Suddenly I'm bright and breezy?
Because of all the wonderful and new, things I'm
learning about you
Day by Day!
-Song from the movie musical, The King and I

Chapter 27

There's No Place Like Home!

Glinda, the Voice of Wisdom Appears

From the spirit realm, Glinda once again floats towards Dorothy in her mystical pink orb and steps out.[1] Dorothy immediately asks her if she will and can help her. Dorothy had been so needy for so long. The majority of the time she depended on others in order to succeed. This was an important factor as she was growing into maturity. She was now realizing that her heart was becoming healthy and whole. The Spirit of heaven had now become integrated with Dorothy's mind and fearful heart. Glinda tells her she doesn't need to be helped anymore and she has always had the power to go back to Kansas. But she had to learn it for herself.

As I studied the book of Romans, I learned that our sinful nature had been crucified with Christ and we were dead to it. In its place we have received the divine nature of God! It said we were no longer children of wrath by nature but children of promise and favor because of God's nature. We are no longer children of the unenlightened dark world but children of the enlightened kingdom of God's dear Son. Our old nature has been exchanged through Christ and He has placed the ruby slippers upon our feet. Dorothy had to walk the path of realization about who she was as a new creation, which took a great effort, many trials and tribulations, taking many years. The truth dawned on her that she was becoming more heav-

---

1 (LeRoy & Fleming, 1939). In the book, Dorothy and her friends visit Glinda who helps her find her way back to Kansas.

enly minded due to heaven's nature which had been placed within her, causing her to be more "earthly good!"

I have now become a completed LGBT. I went from gay to saint, not comparing myself to someone like a Mother Theresa, but just being me and how Christ works through my life. Jesus is the one who calls us saints by living through us! I'm just an "ain't" and Jesus is the S, which equals "Saint." I am transformed from LGBT to L.over of G.od B.eing T.rue. I am a completed L.G.B.T.! Jesus has become the seventh color of my former six-colored rainbow!

Taking an example from a spiritual book, not based entirely on the Bible, there is a bestselling author named John Eckhardt who wrote a book called *The Power of Now*. He shares about spiritual transformation from earthly ego identities and resulting behaviors of what he calls no ego or no self. This self along with everyone in the world is made up of illusory identities that come from the philosophies and darkened understanding of the world. The apostle Paul said the same in that he was no longer his old ego self. He went on to say that it was now Christ living through him. He also stated that he was crucified to the world and the world was crucified to him. Paul was a murderous sinner who became a saint. He had God's heart for the LGBT community in Corinth, Greece. He said they were saved and transformed in the name of Jesus through the charismatic power of God. Gays became saints, and LGBT's became L.overs of G.od B.eing T.rue through Paul's gospel message and this message is the good news of Jesus Christ. In the end, as it is written, "Every knee will bow and every tongue will confess that Jesus Christ is Lord." (Philippians 2:10) I'm so thankful that I have willingly bowed my knee now rather than out of fear and remorse when it's too late.

Home to "My Father, Who Art in Heaven"

When I began to pray the Lord's Prayer with my hands raised in the air at the Hollywood Gay Pride Parade in 1983, I personalized it by saying "My Father" instead of saying "Our Father" as Jesus prayed. My true heavenly Father found me which caused me to find Him. I was no longer fatherless in my mind. The prayer goes on to say "Thy will be done on earth as it is in heaven." I didn't realize that my earthen vessel, meaning my soul and spirit, needed a transformation from heaven itself. This was exemplified by the ruby slippers being placed upon my feet as well as the Holy Spirit being infused within me. My heart and mind needed a revelation and an evolution in order to become a revolution.

Rainbow Transformation

Dorothy became a "Reign-bow Rising" from the storms of her inner life. Jesus was the Reign-bow Resurrection. He became her Rainbow God with all seven colors in place. This Rainbow God not only guided Dorothy over the rainbow but helped her pass through the trials, temptations, and tests of the Yellow Brick Road journey. Dorothy became transformed into the very rainbow colors of God's divine nature mixed with her integrated self. She was now completed enough to bring the Reign-bow Revelation to those she loved.

An Angel is Sent

In the 80's the LGBT community was dancing and seemingly praying to the song "Send me an Angel" sung by a group called Real Life. Dorothy has become one of those angels God has brought from one side of the rainbow to the other and who has real life to share. Jesus says He is the real Way, the real Truth and the real Life!

Dorothy Goes Back to Her Own

Dorothy is now instructed by Glinda to tap her shoes three times to go back home. As she does she wakes from her dream, which was actually a spiritual reality. The real world of the heavenly Oz was now coming back to the dream world of Kansas. Dorothy was now able to help others awaken from their dream world and rise up so that the light of Christ would shine upon them.

Josh and Steve become Completed LGBT's!

In my new blossoming of love, life and the power of God that emerged after coming out of relapse recovery, I prayer walked for those on the downtown streets of my Kansas–Spokane. I let God put all the suffering homeless, youths, addicts and LGBT people in my heart for many hours five days a week. God led me to start a downtown church in an art gallery and I called it "Higher Power Church."

A couple of young men walked in and introduced themselves. One of them shared with me that they were homeless. They said that a friend of theirs had told them about us and we would help them without making them feel condemned about their "gay marriage" status. They both shared they were afraid to step foot into our church because of the fears of being rejected and told they were in sin. I was overjoyed they trusted their friend and courageously came in. I, of all people, would have no reason to put them down. They said they were living on the streets and that were hungry. So we joyfully and lovingly gave what money we had to them to get food. I gave them both tender hugs and felt God's special, chosen love for them. A grandma, named Marlene, saw this happen and came right over to give them some money and hugs as well.

They were so touched that they came Sunday night to help us out and then again the next Saturday to Higher Power Church. They asked if they could receive Jesus at the end of the service. Hello!! Absolutely. They wanted to receive prayer at the same time, but I shared with them that to receive Jesus as Lord and Savior, it needed to be an individual personal commitment for the rest of one's life whether the other person made that commitment or not. They both agreed and each received prayer alone with God.

When Josh verbally prayed before the church congregation to ask Jesus into his heart, to be his Savior and Lord, he fell out under the power of God, while speaking in new tongues! While he was having a supernatural encounter with Jesus on the floor, Stephen did the same thing and asked Jesus to be his personal Lord and Savior. When he did, he also fell to the ground under God's power. He also received the baptism of the Holy Spirit with the evidence of speaking in tongues! When they arose from their spiritual trances, they each shared a heavenly vision God gave to them.

Josh's Vision

Josh shared the vision of himself kneeling at the very feet of Jesus. He said that Jesus was glowing with a heavenly light and placed a special crown upon his head. Then he turned sideways and floated up into the air above Jesus and became as light as Jesus was.

Stephen's Vision

Stephen, after rising from his encounter with God on the floor, shared the vision that he had with Jesus. He said that he saw himself as the good thief that was crucified on the cross next to Jesus as is written in the gospels. He turned to Jesus on His cross, and asked Him if he would remember Him when He went back to His Kingdom.

In the gospel story in the book of John, Jesus told the penitent thief after he made that friendship request, that he (the thief) would be in Paradise with Him that day. To Stephen, Jesus didn't tell him that he'd be in Paradise that day, but took him into a Paradise vision, and there he was in this beautiful garden paradise with Jesus, which was a very beautiful place...more beautiful than this earth could ever be.

Vision Interpretations

I helped to interpret each of their visions. This was new to them. They'd never seen Jesus with them at all! They were even afraid to come to Jesus' churches. They were afraid of Jesus because of some of His followers and they way they can often be treated by other people

Josh's Crown

I shared with Josh that there are different crowns that God has for us. One crown that we receive from Psalm 103, is the crown of compassion. Jesus also crowned him as part of His Royal Family, no longer a gay homeless man...but a Saint..a L.over of G.od B.eing T.rue. When he rose in the air above Jesus, turning as light as Jesus was, this represented his rising to greater heights and no longer being conformed to the world, its Identities, philosophies and ideologies, but Into the image and likeness of Christ.

Stephen's Paradise Garden

I shared with Stephen that his vision represented a special friendship with Jesus. Jesus didn't tell him how bad he was. Rather, He took him "straight up" to paradise in a vision. Josh repented by turning His heart to Jesus, not feeling bad about his past and having to grovel for acceptance. In the vision, he was a thief, meaning he had sins in his life, like we all do and was spiritually dead as a consequence of sin. The Bible says that we were dead in transgressions and sins, but made alive through the righteousness and blood of Jesus Christ!

Shortly after their salvations, infilling of the spirit and visions from God, the three of us were invited to our friend's party. Kathryn's hotel room where she was having a Bridesmaids party. I noticed a jacuzzi! It holds water, which for me means a baptism opportunity! We decided to hold a water baptism for Josh and Stephen. When Josh went into the water, he had a spiritual encounter with God on the feeling level and when Stephen came out of the water, he saw a vision of heavenly light, similar to an aura all around us. We're horses of a different color, so our baptisms are out of the box also.

These young men went from gay to saint. Each of them became L.overs of G.od B.eing T.rue. They both continue to love the Lord to this day after two years and are walking in faith in their Yellow Brick Road journey to spiritual transformation, power and love in Christ. It won't be as hard for them on the journey as it was for me because they have a safe place and a loving Christian family to walk with them in love, truth, gentleness and patience.

An Invitation

Here is an invitation not to change, but to surrender, put your trust, either for the first time or again, and follow Him. Don't worry about His followers, just follow Him and he'll complete the good work He began in you. Read an easy version of the New Testament. I like the NIV (New International Version) and the *Message Bible*. One of my favorite new versions, even though I like most all of them is called the *Mirror Bible*. It highlights spiritual identities in Christ. It's amazing. God will guide you to books, people, church groups, conferences and healing seminars. There is so much out there for you from God to help you on the journey. Don't give up! Don't give in! Know thyself! I pray that God will enlighten the eyes of your heart to know who you are in Christ, who God is, and the destiny upon your life. The Holy Spirit places you in church families—not perfect ones, of course, but ones that will have hearts to nurture you and aid you on your path. Similarly to Josh and Steve, you may be afraid to step foot in a church either for your first time, or ever again, especially if you've been used or abused. Not everyone is bad, and Jesus has many loving followers who are waiting to embrace LGBT with great love, patience, kindness and guidance. I can't tell you where to go, but ask God to guide you to green pastures and still waters to restore your soul. He will! He promises that. If you've been hurt by the followers of Jesus, remember that Dorothy was too, but it all worked for something greater in her heart. She became Love. I will be writing a Study Guide to go along with this story you and others that you feel safe with can work through your own personal journey. Be looking for it!

What satan, the spirit of witchcraft worked against her through life in her Kansas and afterwards through empty fear and religion, discovered reality as it truly is. Her illusions faded and she understood who she was and what was going on behind the scenes. She got her power back and was no longer a victim, an orphan or confused. She became a L.over of G.od B.eing T.rue. She didn't go "straight." She went Saint! Straight up! And love came into order within her as she sought the kingdom of God and all His righteousness.

Only God has the power to change us, so don't worry. Just walk with Him and don't give up. The reward is immensely greater than any suffering through this arduous and joyous adventure.

A Simple Prayer to Pray from Your Heart

The key steps are to believe in your heart that Jesus rose from the dead, and confess Him as Lord. (Romans 10:9) Thus, you shall be saved and you will receive the gift of the Holy Spirit! Follow the Yellow brick Road! God allows U-turns. A righteous man may fall many times but rises again. Don't give up. Don't give in. Walk in the Spirit and be filled with the Spirit with an inner melody of gratitude singing in your heart. This is who you are as a L.over of G.od B.eing T.rue. You are favored and chosen. You who are reading this are God's chosen baby! Grow up into the fullness of Christ in you. Don't exchange the glorious riches of your inheritance in Christ for the fool's gold and false riches the world and its vain philosophies offer.

You are a bluebird over the rainbow. Fly way up high and be found there! L.ove G.od B.e T.rue!

Unto the church of God which is at Corinth
(including all of the L.ove G.od B.e T.rue members),
to them that are sanctified in Christ Jesus, called to be
saints...Grace to you and peace from God our Father
and the Lord Jesus Christ.
1 Corinthians 1:2-3

A Prayer to Return Home, Where the Heart is

If you want a personal relationship or want to renew your relationship with God and His purpose for your life, here is a simple prayer you can pray...

Father, I know that I have strayed from You and my sins have separated me from fellowship with You. I am truly sorry, and now I want to turn away from anything in my life that is keeping me distant and away from You. Please forgive me, and keep me from being distracted by anything and anyone that would keep me from Your love and the purposes You have for my life. I believe that Your son, Jesus Christ died for my sins, was resurrected from the dead, is alive, and hears my prayer. I invite Jesus to become the Lord of my life, to rule and reign in my heart from this day forward. Please send your Holy Spirit to help me obey You and to do Your will for the rest of my life. In Jesus' name I pray, Amen.

Bibliography

Baum, Frank. *The Wonderful Wizard of Oz*. Salt Lake City: The Project Gutenburg, 2008, EBook #55.

Lindsay, Scott. "1 Corinthians 1:1-9." RPM, Volume 12, Number 12 (March 21 to March 27, 2010): http://old.thirdmill.org/new-files/sco_lindsay/sco_lindsay.1Cor.002.pdf. Web. Accessed July 2017.

The Wizard of Oz. Dir. Victor Fleming. Metro-Goldwyn-Mayer (MGM), 1939. Film.

Angel's Poems

Who Am I?

I've done gay things...but am not gay.
I've done bi things...but am not bi.
I've done straight things...but am not straight.
I've tried some-things, but am not some-thing
I haven't tried all things...so am not all things.
I am a soul that was born to the world,
I got lost in the Warp, like everyone has
And had to re-find who I was.
Who was I before I was born...before I was knit in the womb?
The answer did lie from the Source of all things..
To the Source in the Mystical Room.
I'm not what I thought..
Or you think...
Or they
And neither are you...
You think you're ok!
A New Birth I've had
Through the Womb of the bad
From darkness to light
And from gladness to sad.
What is the title you have for me?
Is it Gay,
Straight?
Or bi?
Or is it deceived?
The only name I have for myself...
Is Me!
And Me is I,
And I am,
And Why?
'Cause Love put me here,
And for me Love did die.
And Love then did rise

From the Depth to the skies
And carried my heart
From the Warp and the Lies
Straight to the Realm of the Father of Lights.
I am a Revolution
Of a New Evolution
I am Transforming
From the Night to the Morning
From a Worm to the Wings
Like a Rainbow that Sings
A Harmonious Mode
On a Yellow Brick Road.

Mystical AIDS

Behold the Son, O' Positive One
Look to the Light,
As you pass through the Night
HIV
Is
Higher in Vision
AIDS
Is
Acquired in-tune Divinity Syndrome
HIV can be Positive
If by it you choose to Be-live
Seek and Find
Til the Door of your Mind
Enlightens and Brightens
Your View of Mankind
What is it to truly Live?
Is it Length, is it Height,
Is it Breadth, or just Width?
Transforming Mistake
Unto MYSTIC
Material

To Simplistic
On Eagles Wings
Prepare Ye to Soar
From Dying to Living
The Alchemist's Door
Every Question
Veils an Answer
Are you Human?
Or are you DANCER?
Are you Earthly?
Or Eternal GLANCER?
Don't stop Short...
Traversing the Stars
While Feeling the Scars
Soar past the Clouds
Dissolve Prison Bars
Let Go
And Ascend
While the Staircase Descends
A Secret is Speaking
Lose not Heart
Persevere in You're Reaching
The Cloud of Unknowing
Will Whisper to You
You were Born for this Day
Love's Coming to You!

Written by Angel Willson Dec. 1st on World AID's Day

A Question

Transformation? Experimentation?
Essence or Events?
The Beginning or the End?
Am I willing to Transcend?
Death brings life

Dark brings death
And Shades to light
Higher to the Center
From the Lower to the Heights
Hiding in the Light
Expressing in the Dark
Laughing in the Pain
And Weeping in the Park
Never ending...Circle Pretending
Lies are Good and
Light is Bad
Inside Out?
Or
Outside In?
Am I the One?
Or One Within?
Is Love just Hate in Theatre's Stage?
Is there a Star...
A Mystique Sage?
BEHOLD, I Seek,
Behold, I sink
Behold, I think
Behold, I shrink
I Feel A Breeze
It's Warm.
It's Cool.
What is Real?
Am I a Fool?
Am I Indifferent?
Or am I Different?
Am I a Wave?
Or am I Sea?
The Truth will be known when You will See.

Written by Angel Willson July 2010

Meet Angel Willson

Angel Willson is a minister based in Spokane, Washington. For over three decades he has served as a worship leader, prophetic psalmist, evangelist, missionary, pastor, teacher. As this, his first book reveals, Angel experienced salvation in 1983 at the Hollywood Gay Pride Parade. Since then he has walked through a beautiful, fantastic and arduous journey. Angel often moves out in spiritual singing that many share bring the tangible experience of the presence of God. Many times when Angel is either preaching, teaching or psalming with his guitar and/or accompanied by music minstrels, people have received visions, prophetic songs and prophetic words, healings, salvation experiences and spiritual ecstacies of diverse kinds.

Angel has been called an apostle of love, an evangelist and a spiritual teacher by prophets and ministers. Through his life journey of following Jesus he has been trained by God and personally influenced by many leaders. He was invited as a 2 week guest to minister at Timothy House, a ministry of Times Square Church in New York City under the leadership of David Wilkerson. At a general service during that visit, David Wilkerson prayed publicly over Angel that he would become a firebrand in America!

Angel has ministered in Russia, Israel, Mexico, South Korea, England, East and South Africa as well as throughout the United States. He has also been on local, national and international television as well as radio and diverse media outlets.

Angel operates apostolically in his region, starting and cultivating regional prophetic oriented fellowships, innovative downtown inner city evangelism outreaches and raising up mission teams. Angel has worked in ministry partnership with Grace Wilson (pictured here with Angel) since 1991. He developed an inner city Light Club for two years called The Rainbow Electric House of Prayer in his hometown with spiritual flowing music ministry, light shows, open mic, outdoor barbecues, clothing giveaway and food. Angel is very creative with outreaches to the poor, homeless, orphans and people with various addictions.

Angel has been led by God to Southern California to work with Meri Crouley Ministries to awaken God's people to the harvest through the Media on different projects. He is also working on a special project with Meri, who is developing a movie about a young hippie named Lonnie Frisbee who struggled with his sexuality, but was mightily used of God to bring the Jesus people movement to Calvary Chapel in Costa Mesa in the early 70's. Lonnie was a miracle worker and power evangelist leading thousands of hippies to Christ and was a catalyst of worldwide charismatic denominations. Angel is a Lonnie Frisbee type—fun, a little crazy, and empowered by the Holy Spirit with signs, wonders and miracles that follow him. Angel also, like Lonnie Frisbee, was exposed to the AIDS virus in the early days. Angel is now a sign and wonder. He is alive 30+ years later. He is still HIV positive, but prefers to call himself JC Positive!

If you would like to invite Angel to speak and minister, you can contact him at:

Angel WillSon
P.O. Box 10275
Spokane, WA 99209
dorothysclub@yahoo.com

Dorothy's Club

Angel is the founder of Dorothy's Club found online at:
www.dorothysclub.org

This is a developing web site that will include blogs, form to contact Angel, book ordering and various resources, events and inspiring stories from Dorothy's Club friends.

www.dorothysclub.org

Made in the USA
Middletown, DE
28 July 2019